Value-Added Records Management

764

JY 22 '94

Information Resources Center
AMERICAN SOCIETY FOR
INDUSTRIAL SECURITY
1625 Prince Street
Alexandria, VA 22314

HF
5736
.S25
1992

Value-Added

Records

Management

PROTECTING CORPORATE ASSETS
AND REDUCING BUSINESS RISKS

KAREN L. SAMPSON

Q

Quorum Books

New York • Westport, Connecticut • London

Library of Congress Cataloging-in-Publication Data

Sampson, Karen L.
    Value-added records management : protecting corporate assets and
reducing business risks / Karen L. Sampson.
        p.   cm.
    Includes bibliographical references (p.) and index.
    ISBN 0-89930-676-4 (alk. paper)
    1. Business records—Management. 2. Information resources
management. I. Title.
HF5736.S25 1992
651.5—dc20   91–45710

British Library Cataloguing in Publication Data is available.

Copyright © 1992 by Karen L. Sampson

All rights reserved. No portion of this book may be
reproduced, by any process or technique, without the
express written consent of the publisher.

Library of Congress Catalog Card Number: 91–45710
ISBN: 0-89930-676-4

First published in 1992

Quorum Books, One Madison Avenue, New York NY 10010
An imprint of Greenwood Publishing Group, Inc.

Printed in the United States of America

The paper used in this book complies with the
Permanent Paper Standard issued by the National
Information Standards Organization (Z39.48–1984).

10 9 8 7 6 5 4 3 2 1

Contents

Preface

Every business that has employees, customers, or tax bills has record-keeping requirements. As a company's memory, records and information help respond to top management concerns about:

- efficiencies and costs
- liability issues
- legislation and compliance
- catastrophes

Records and information are an element of a company's infrastructure in that they support and protect the business. They trace the path of important business decisions and transactions as they show evidence of compliance with laws and government regulations.

How well records and information are managed determines their impact on an enterprise and its employees, customers, and other stakeholders. We need information systems to retain and recall essential information at will, at the lowest cost possible. But an explosion of information and office technologies is creating a crisis for top management. Today's office environment is populated with a number of independent information systems, and no single system will satisfy the increasingly complex and demanding information needs of today's marketplace.

In today's competitive, regulated, and litigious environment, records management is a necessary cost of doing business, not unlike personnel management or legal and accounting services. Yet few executives know who in their organization is managing the company's information or how well it is being managed.

The records and information management concept is not new. What is new is the nature of the beast. Our information-intensive society is exerting pressures on business to produce and process information faster than ever before. The traditional concept that records management has to do with filing and records centers must be laid to rest. Today's records and information management is far more sophisticated, as it encompasses multimedia formats and a wide range of legal issues.

We have let the arteries of our important information systems become clogged with excess and obsolete information, and more and more information is being created and retained in a variety of formats. Information growth and fast-paced changes in technologies are putting information out of the control of even the most well-intentioned business. We have mountains of paper files and computer printouts. Rolls of microfilm and stacks of microfiche are filling boxes and cabinets. Audio and video tapes are hidden away in corners and desk drawers. Diskettes are scattered throughout offices, computer tapes are consuming warehouse space, and optical disks are filling cabinets. Today, we also face new information systems in the form of voice and video.

We need a new way of thinking about our information resources. Instead of focusing our resources on the various forms of records, the focus should be on the content of our records. Records and information are valuable assets in that they provide evidence of a company's conduct and activities to protect its rights and obligations. They also may become a liability. What distinguishes between their existence as an asset or as a liability is the judicious control and protection of records and information.

Maintaining the right records for the right time and disposing of the right records at the right time is a perpetual and delicate balancing act. When that balance tips to one side or another, worst-case scenarios may be costly inefficiencies and senseless losses in court or government proceedings. Basic records and information management practices identify the valuable and legally required records in all media to be retained and protected in order to meet legal and business obligations. Those records no longer needed are destroyed to prevent them from becoming a direct drain on revenues or an unnecessary exposure to liabilities. The fewer and better records that are retained are organized and preserved in a manner that improves efficiencies, reduces costs, and prevents losses.

PURPOSE OF THIS BOOK

We are a long way from exploiting the opportunities and benefits that records and information have to offer. The gap between records management practice and its potential is widening, much like the gap between new technologies and worker capabilities. Contributing to this gap are new office technologies that fragment the information systems of an enterprise and the lack of support from top management.

The purpose of this work is to raise levels of awareness regarding the various roles of records and information management in business today. Executives, professionals, and managers are the individuals who will make a difference regarding how our information resources impact a business. They are ultimately responsible for the design and administration of a records and information management program—and for whether it adds value to an enterprise or becomes a liability.

This book is intended only for general information purposes. Discussions of issues are general in nature and must not be construed as providing legal advice. Any suggestions offered are based on a presumption of working within the law. Neither the author nor the publisher advocates covert or illegal behavior or impropriety. The reader is encouraged to consult with an attorney concerning specific circumstances and legal questions. Records and information management program development must be thought out carefully. Organizational differences and the advice of legal counsel determine the final interpretations and guidelines for record-keeping within the law to protect the enterprise.

This book provides examples of how a comprehensive records and information management program will add value to a business. The focus is primarily on applications for external purposes and on the effective management of records for those applications. A more detailed discussion of internal business uses of records and information is better covered in a separate work.

The basic records and information management principles presented are applicable to most sizes and types of business. Scenarios used throughout the book to illustrate specific points are based on realistic situations. Those scenarios describing an actual company use the true name of that company. Otherwise, no company name or a fictitious name is used in a scenario to illustrate a situation.

Each chapter covers different aspects of a comprehensive records and information program. Individual records and information management principles are repeated in more than one chapter when they relate to more than one program element. The issues discussed are by their very nature interrelated or interdependent, so references to relevant chapters are used where appropriate.

The chapter overviews provided here may be of assistance to the reader who wishes to select individual chapters for separate study.

The first three chapters illustrate the role of records and information in various business activities and situations. Chapter 1, "Guilty until Proven Innocent," discusses a number of situations in which proper record-keeping practices are necessary for an organization to defend itself. Chapter 2, "Preservation of Legal Rights and Business Assets," describes several conditions under which proper record-keeping practices are necessary for a business to protect itself from harm or losses.

Employers generally are on the defense regarding employee safety and health, employment actions, and privacy issues. An employer also has certain rights regarding protection of its assets. Record-keeping practices related to both of these aspects of employment are covered in Chapter 3, "Employer Rights and Responsibilities."

Chapter 4, "A Day in Court," is more specific on a company's rights and obligations regarding its records in the litigation process. There may be serious consequences for a company with too many records, too few records, or records that are not considered trustworthy.

How well—or how poorly—a business manages its records and information will have an impact on the bottom line. Chapter 5, "The Bottom Line," suggests ways that a well-designed, comprehensive records and information management program can provide a competitive edge through improved productivity, reduced costs, and loss prevention.

Responsive information systems enable a business to respond quickly to changing business conditions and to then expectations of a wide range of constituents. Chapter 6, "The Roles of Records in Corporate Change," discusses various roles of records and information in business growth, ownership changes, restructurings, and other business changes.

Chapters 7, 8, and 9 define sensitive, valuable, and vital records that are to be protected from a number of threats. The potential consequences of inadequate protection are described in Chapter 7, "Sensitive and Valuable Records and Information," and Chapter 9, "Records Vital to a Business." Chapter 8, "Information Security," and Chapter 9 suggest methods to prevent or reduce business losses resulting from unauthorized disclosure and other records and information losses.

As much as 50 percent of a company's records may be true liabilities in that they have no financial, operational, or legal value. Keeping valueless records is an unnecessary burden and senseless exposure to potential liabilities, but indiscriminate disposal of records may have even more serious consequences. Chapter 10, "Records Retention and Disposition," explores a number of business and legal considerations that support records retention decisions.

Computer and microform information systems increasingly are being used to speed retrieval and consolidate growing volumes of business records. Without appropriate controls and a proper business focus, an organization may end up with expensive technologies sitting around with no real productive value or purpose. The best return on investments in records and information systems is realized by the appropriate design and integration of information systems, as discussed in Chapter 11, "Integrating Media Choices."

A comprehensive records and information program necessitates interactions among a number of different business functions. Chapter 12, "Organization and Staffing for the Records Function," describes the elements of a records and information management program, and how a program may be administered within an organization.

Chapter 13, "The Challenges Ahead," summarizes issues previously discussed and introduces additional management issues facing business today and in the future. Few businesses had a smoothly functioning paper records system before they began to take on microfilm, computer, and other information systems. New perspectives, expertise, and tools are necessary to exploit fully the records and information management capabilities to provide better information at lower costs—regardless of the record form.

LOOKING AHEAD

It is the wise executive who recognizes the roles of records and information management in protecting a business and improving organizational effectiveness—before a crisis of crippling litigation, overcrowded facilities, or a devastating fire makes it painfully obvious. To maintain records as an asset and a resource, rather than a burden, they must be organized and controlled from the time of their creation to their ultimate disposition.

Needed for the long term is an enterprise-wide records and information system that is easy to use, easy to manage, and easy to change. It must be endorsed by top management, corporate attorneys, and the managers of all existing and future information systems. The transformation from today's fragmented systems into a comprehensive program will evolve over time. No enterprise has developed the perfect records program on the first attempt, though a handful of companies have come close to doing so.

Records and information management today is both simple and complex, but an informed and common-sense approach will make the job a little easier. The same foresight and commitment necessary to develop a successful business will be necessary to build a records and information program that supports and protects the enterprise. It could make the difference between mere survival and prosperity.

Value–Added
Records
Management

Guilty until Proven Innocent

No matter how diligently a business tries to identify, understand, and comply with the law, it is inevitable that it will experience some type of government investigation or litigation during its lifetime. In today's litigating society, attorneys are kept busy filing claims and defending their clients against claims involving other businesses, the government, and individuals.

Written contracts and litigators have been eroding the sense of fair play and long-term business relationships so valued in yesterday's business environment. Instead of handshakes and negotiation, differences are settled by attorneys and juries. A growing minority of companies are finding it easier to sue a rival than to compete on a level playing field.

The expenses and losses related to litigation and government investigation traditionally have been viewed as a cost of doing business. But they are only the tip of the iceberg. Whether a company is right or wrong, the legal costs and any related losses could alter the fate of a business. Even a single lawsuit can be potentially ruinous in terms of the time and money spent, damaged company image, and any adverse ruling.

As a result of the explosion of lawsuits, the costs of insuring against them are skyrocketing, along with the jury awards. Estimated annual costs of out-of-court settlements, attorney and expert witness fees, and jury awards in the United States are close to $200 billion. Today, companies are paying product liability insurance premiums that are triple what they paid in the 1970's. The high costs for an organization to defend itself force many businesses to settle even when they are innocent of the charges.

Recent changes in corporate crime penalties and the prospect of imprisonment have become new incentives to anticipate the need for a proper defense against any criminal charges. Under new federal sentencing guidelines for corporations, lesser fines will apply if a firm establishes and enforces procedures aimed at keeping it in compliance with federal laws.

Government interest in business and its records is expressed through statutes, regulations, statutes of limitations, and various rules and procedures established to protect the public interest and to assess taxes. Government requirements to routinely report information are an effort to monitor business activities for compliance with the law. The Internal Revenue Service (IRS), Environmental Protection Agency (EPA), and Occupational Health and Safety Administration (OSHA) are among the numerous government agencies intent on monitoring business in the areas of:

- environment
- health and safety
- securities
- insurance
- banking
- products and consumer protection

Among the many ways for a business to work within the law to protect itself is proper record-keeping. Record-keeping can assist in compliance with the law, demonstrate that compliance, and enable a company to avoid unnecessary charges. But not every business today is fully aware of the role of records in various business conduct issues or its legal responsibilities and rights regarding records and information. As a result, most businesses do not do much in terms of records management until they are hit with a major lawsuit or government investigation. By then, it may be too costly and time-consuming to try to straighten out the dilemma— and it may be too late for protection in that particular instance.

Any business is vulnerable to claims or charges, even when there is no validity to them. Current and accurate documentation can minimize the expense and burden of a defense. Regardless of whether a government requirement exists to create and maintain certain records, a business should maintain records in order to show compliance with a law and to help prevent unnecessary charges and claims against the business.

ENVIRONMENTAL ISSUES

Business conduct issues that are of more sensitivity to the public, such as claims of environmental violations, often place a company in a position of being guilty until proven innocent. Similar to cases involving the word of one person against another, proper record-keeping may be critical in this uphill battle.

Environmental affairs have long been a priority for heavy industry. Today, environmental impact is considered in product development, manufacturing, packaging, and marketing throughout many other industries. Even the Walt Disney Company was fined for illegal dumping of hazardous cleaning solvents used at Disneyland.

Any business that uses chemicals or discharges contaminated water and air into the environment is vulnerable to charges of environmental violations. Toxic substances are common in cleaning agents, copy machines, refrigeration equipment, batteries, insulating materials, and more. The toxic substances list for the Clean Air Act, the Clean Water Act, and other environmental laws includes close to 200 pollutants.

The regulations are not always clear, and the base of knowledge regarding hazardous and toxic materials is not always adequate. The proliferation of government record-keeping requirements is an attempt to develop appropriate controls through more knowledge.

The 1990 Clean Air Act is more than 600 pages in length. After the Act goes into effect in 1994, businesses will be required to complete forms necessary for permits. The EPA estimates that the cost to U.S. companies to complete the forms over five years will be $300 million. Critics say that cost will be higher because people will have to complete the forms more than once to get them right, as a result of such a large number of new rules.

Additional information disclosure requirements exist regarding hazardous materials and environmental problems.

- OSHA's Hazard Communication Standard and the states' Workers-Right-To-Know laws require informing workers of hazardous materials.

- The Securities and Exchange Commission (SEC) requires public companies to disclose any potential and quantifiable financial liabilities regarding environmental obligations.

- Violation of a 1986 chemical reporting law may be a fine of $50,000 a day.

Individuals who willingly and knowingly pollute are being held personally responsible for environmental damages. Criminal charges are resulting in jail sentences and personal fines of up to $10,000 a day. Business indictments for environmental crimes reached an all-time high by 1991, when felony convictions of owners and corporate managers for hazardous waste violations resulted in sentences totalling 21 years of prison time and fines of more than $18 million.

Business increasingly must bear the full brunt of environmental damage costs. The government is making efforts to hold property owners responsible, and insurance companies are requesting environmental audits or are excluding most environmental claims.

With liability for hazardous waste cleanup falling on the land owner, banks and other lenders often require an environmental audit before accepting a property as loan collateral or before foreclosing on a property. Even if contamination occurred years prior to involvement of the land owner, the current land owner may be held responsible for any necessary cleanup.

In a landmark Maryland case, a bank foreclosed on a property that was worth $350,000. Before it was all said and done, the bank eventually wound up paying $550,000 for an environmental cleanup of the property.

Ignorance of the law or ignorance of contamination will be no excuse.

The House of Good Intentions hired a painting contractor to sandblast old paint from a two-story tank. Neither the contractor nor the contracting company tested the old paint to see if it contained lead—which, in fact, it did. The contractor disposed of a large volume of the waste in a non-hazardous waste dump, and it failed to clean up all paint chips at the site. Eventually, contaminants leached into the soil and into ground water. The contracting company became liable for the clean-up and is attempting to force the contractor to share some of the responsibility for dumping toxic waste at a non-hazardous waste landfill based on its contracting agreement.

The environmental services industry is growing by leaps and bounds in response to the demands for environmental audits. The resulting data and records attest to a company's efforts and good faith.

Each phase of an environmental audit involves record-keeping. In Phase I, there is a site inspection and an extensive search of federal, state, and local records for evidence of past property owner(s), registration of underground storage tanks, any environmental violations, and so on. Additional records may be created throughout Phases II and III for sampling and analysis, and any violations are reported to the appropriate government authorities. Site remediation, Phase IV, also requires creation of documentation.

In addition to environmental audit records, information to be recorded or reported regarding hazardous substances and environmental impact may include:

- logs of toxic materials
- periodic environmental assessments
- regular monitoring of air, ground and surface water, and emissions
- solid waste permitting and management
- fuel management program
- accident prevention measures
- incident reports to the Department of Transportation, OSHA, EPA, or other appropriate regulatory agency
- efforts to eliminate or reduce emissions
- remediation and reclamation efforts

Unfortunately, accurate and complete environmental record-keeping is no guarantee against charges of violations. The Department of Justice has attempted to reassure companies that they will not be criminally prosecuted if a violation revealed in an audit is reported to the proper regulatory authorities and is corrected in a reasonable time period. Records of good faith efforts are better than no records at all.

PRODUCT LIABILITY AND PERSONAL INJURY

As new laws, regulations, and court decisions favor the consumer, the scope of consumer responsibility is narrowing and corporate liability is expanding. A poor economy and media hype about successful claims are contributing to a growing number of claims initiated by individuals against business. It may be easier and very lucrative to sue when an impersonal corporation or insurance company can be compelled to pay. Many consumers are jumping on the bandwagon, driven by greed or a compelling need to place blame somewhere other than on fate or on themselves.

Though cases involving big money tend to be decided by an appeals court, the increasing number of multi-million-dollar jury verdicts could be the sign of a rising tide against business. Plaintiffs are asking not only for damages to compensate for losses, but also for punitive damages. Nearly half of the total damages paid in medical and product liability cases consists of awards for pain and suffering above and beyond lost wages, medical costs, and other real expenses. Until the U.S. Supreme Court is asked to review the issue of a cap on pain and suffering, business is vulnerable to heavy losses in the handful of states that have struck down such a limit as of this writing.

Most cases are settled out of court to avoid suffering losses in a trial and the expense of an appeal. The fear of civil liability also has high costs to the U.S. economy. Innovation and research may be stifled and foreign competitiveness may be reduced along with the workforce. Products are withdrawn from the market because of prohibitive insurance costs or because insurance cannot be bought at any price. Prices are raised to cover the cost of modifying production methods and materials or skyrocketing insurance premiums.

> Costly and burdensome restrictions are quickly imposed by new laws after injuries or deaths, sometimes without due consideration of their reasonableness. In the wake of the 1982 case of cyanide-laced Tylenol capsules, the industry and consumers are paying for new product packaging design. The new packaging succeeds in keeping the elderly from its contents, but it still cannot prevent consumer terrorism.

Hot areas of litigation today are medical malpractice and product liability. Even pharmaceutical and aircraft manufacturers of federally approved products are targets. There are no clear standards for well-intentioned companies to follow and thus be assured they will not be sued—no matter how exemplary their behavior. Though a company is in compliance with government standards, there is no guarantee against punitive damages.

Victims use products in ways other than their intended uses, or while under the influence of drugs or alcohol. In one case, a couple sued a major retailer and several suppliers for injuries suffered when they used an outdoor cooking grill indoors. They claimed that the warnings on the grill against the product's use indoors should have been written in larger letters. Rather than go through the expense of court and risks of a jury sympathetic to the plaintiffs, the defendants settled for $4.8 million.

Liability for durable products also may put a company at a disadvantage.

A manufacturer of semiconductors and office equipment purchased a company that had made presses for embossing book covers before the turn of the century. Over the years, many press owners had modified and modernized the presses. However, the new business owner was forced to defend itself against a suit for $700,000 when an operator crushed his fingers in a modified press.

A new strategy of plaintiff attorneys is to file claims against multiple defendants. After an airplane crash, the airline and its manufacturer and suppliers may become defendants. Or when a driver kills someone in an accident when he ran a stop sign, the auto manufacturer, auto parts suppliers, city maintenance department, and others may be dragged into the suit as defendants. These secondary defendants tend to settle more quickly than the primary target, and litigators hope they may offer up damning evidence against the primary target.

The Federal Drug Administration (FDA) and the Federal Trade Commission (FTC) have numerous product regulations intended to protect the consumer. The FDA requires proof that a new drug is safe for consumption before it may be sold to the public. One application for FDA approval of a new drug was a half-ton document of 19,000 pages.

Both the FTC and the FDA began aggressive crackdowns in 1991 on misleading or false claims in product labeling and advertising. When a manufacturer makes claims about its product, such as "low cholesterol content" or "environmentally safe," it must be prepared to show that those claims are true through research, testing, and other documentation.

The FDA also has an interest in tracking controlled substances. Drug distribution records have proven useful when batches of drugs had to be recalled to check for possible contamination, as in the case of cyanide-laced Tylenol capsules.

In a recent court settlement, one drug company agreed to pay a fine of $600,000 as a result of its poor record-keeping on the delivery of product samples to physicians. Sales personnel who delivered the controlled substances in question failed to record accurately and completely the registration numbers of samples distributed. Because the company had already paid fines for other record-keeping violations during the previous decade, the government ordered that the company stop the practice of sales representatives from hand-delivering the samples. In the event of further violations, the company will be ordered to pay an additional $500,000.

In addition to records required by government agencies, other records that may be necessary in a defense against product liability or personal injury claims may include:

- product and material testing results
- production quality control documentation
- equipment and vehicle inspections and maintenance records

As with environmental issues, records of good faith efforts may be better than no records at all for product liability and personal injury claims. However, older documents may be taken out of context, misinterpreted, and used against a defendant. (Chapters 4, "A Day in Court," and 10, "Records Retention and Disposition," provide more detail on the retention and destruction of records.)

Manville Corporation, formerly Johns Manville, was a manufacturer of products made from asbestos. After many years of meeting heavy demands for fire retarding materials in public and government facilities, Manville was the target of liability claims totalling billions of dollars as people developed asbestosis, a lung disease caused by exposure to asbestos.

The company's records retention program had not been implemented over the years, so older documents that legally could have been destroyed years before the lawsuits began were not destroyed. Sources close to the case note that many of the records involved in the suit—dating back to the 1930's—were used by opposing parties to create an impression that Manville knew or should have known that asbestos was hazardous.

To avoid complete ruin of the business, Johns Manville filed Chapter 11 bankruptcy to protect itself from creditors until the claims could be resolved. (The company emerged from reorganization in 1988 as Manville Corporation.) Under the court settlement, Manville initially paid $2.5 billion into a trust fund to cover the claims of current and future victims, and it operates a warehouse of 16 million pages of documents for access by future claimants.

Release of proprietary information during the discovery process also may be hazardous to the health of a company. A business has a right to request nondisclosure or limited disclosure of its trade secrets and other confidential information. Once proprietary information becomes a part of the public record, the company loses future protection of the information as a trade secret. (See Chapters 4, "A Day in Court," and 8, "Records and Information Security," for more information on the discovery process and protective orders.) Efforts to restrict the disclosure of proprietary information—within the boundaries of the law—may become especially important in product and environmental liability claims in order to prevent those documents from becoming readily available to future claimants.

In the first of many product liability lawsuits expected to go to trial, a defendant company requested that its product documents be protected from public view by sealing the court documents. The manufacturer considered, and ruled out, the traditional approach to trade secret protection because it is not always successful in product liability lawsuits where there is a strong presumption of the public's right to know about potential hazards, so all court records should be public. Instead, the defendant turned to copyright law as a rationale to protect its documents. The judge refused the request, ruling that copyright protection "may not be asserted to impede or prevent free use and accessibility of such documents in the context of this litigation."

Rather than risk public disclosure of as many as 8,000 pages of company documents as they would be introduced into evidence, the manufacturer offered a settlement that the plaintiff could not refuse.

Other than the plaintiff's agreement not to disclose any of the thousands of documents exchanged by the parties, the terms of the settlement were undisclosed. The company retains the confidentiality of its proprietary information and is protected from an onslaught of similar suits.

FINANCIAL TRANSACTIONS AND ASSET MANAGEMENT

Record-keeping regarding financial transactions and asset management is a necessity for both internal and external purposes. Laws and regulations applicable to a number of industries and specific transactions also necessitate good record-keeping.

Accounting records and financial statements are used primarily for business management activities and for audited statements. Internal audits may be conducted by a parent company or by a finance, legal, or auditing department. Audits conducted by outside firms generally are for purposes of information disclosure to or review by:

- federal contract compliance auditors
- taxing agencies
- securities regulators
- various state organizations
- regulatory commissions
- private shareholders
- lending institutions and other creditors

The records to be reviewed in an audit may vary from one type of audit to another. Auditors may request anything from invoices and shipping receipts to sales journals and general ledgers. They also may request legal documents that impact the transactions being examined in order to identify any future obligations or debt restrictions.

Publicly traded companies must provide audited financial statements and other information to the SEC. The SEC receives 280,000 separate documents—about 12 million pages—from 11,000 companies every year. The SEC regulations and state securities laws are aimed at providing the public with accurate and full disclosure about securities and stock through registration statements, prospectuses, and other information disclosures.

Former executives of a corporation are facing charges of insider trading and financial fraud. The fraud charges and the $400 million in damages being sought are aimed at former executives, company directors, venture capitalists, and accountants. The SEC claims that the company overstated its income by millions of dollars over more than two years. It charges that the auditor's inventory numbers were altered through the creation of fictitious inventory in transit and by packaging or shipping scrap and bricks as inventory. The executives sold shares of stock based on those inflated figures, making $2.5 million more than the stock was actually worth, and they were paid bonuses based on the inflated financial information.

Foreign branches of Wall Street firms are not exempt from securities laws. They must set up their record-keeping to comply with laws of the United States and other countries.

The SEC censured a New York brokerage firm for failure to keep and provide regulators with records from its Switzerland branch. The branch manager was charged with failing to supervise subordinates while they were committing the alleged violations and was barred from the securities business for a specified period of time.

Private and public franchisors have information disclosure requirements similar to those of corporations regulated by the SEC. State attorneys general and civil suits are targeting franchisors for false and misleading information regarding costs, franchisor expertise and support available, the competition, start-up costs, and so on.

Other businesses with inaccurate records also may be targets for reforms. The credit reporting industry has come under fire in recent years for sloppy record-keeping practices that lead to errors in consumer credit files and the recurrence of errors as a result of poor investigation of complaints about errors. The industry's practices of selling its data on individuals to junk-mailers and to other companies for hiring decisions will be reviewed carefully in the near future.

Information disclosure and accuracy requirements also exist in the area of taxes. The IRS and other tax agencies generally do not define what records must be maintained to support the information reported on tax returns, but the taxpayer has the burden of proof that the claims made on the return are accurate.

Supporting documentation for federal and state income tax returns may include:

- employee payments and tax withholding records
- proof of tax payments
- 1099 forms and supporting documentation
- fixed asset records
- product inventory records
- sales transactions, journals, and tax payments
- check registers

Many other regulatory agencies do not always state that certain records must exist. However, the absence of those records may result in a loss of rights.

The FTC has established time requirements for shipment of mail-order merchandise to buyers. When the seller has no records that show compliance with the regulation, the FTC may presume failure to comply with the time requirement.

Insurance companies often ask a company to provide detailed information and records so they may analyze the degree of risk involved in providing coverage to the company.

Federal banking regulators are filing multi-million-dollar lawsuits against law firms that represented failed banks and thrifts. As a result, many law firms representing banks, savings and loans, and other financial institutions are having difficulty maintaining malpractice insurance. One law firm was asked to provide to the insurance company records on its client financial institutions for the past five to seven years.

Detailed records also may be necessary in the event of litigation or investigation of antitrust charges. Potential mergers, acquisitions, or strategic alliances are reviewed by the Department of Justice or the FTC for possible antitrust violations. SEC requirements also may be applicable if securities or stock transactions are involved. Once a charge is made, the target company will rely heavily on its records to show its innocence.

Antitrust violations, not to be taken lightly, may result in any of the following:

- loss of property or rights
- liability for treble damages
- fines or prison sentences
- court or government supervision of operations
- divestiture of stock or assets or other business relationships

All important decisions that may affect competitive relationships, agreements with suppliers or distributors, acquisitions, and mergers must be documented. It is best to make a record of compliance before—not after—being sued or investigated. These records may document:

- contacts with competitors, customers, and distributors
- events and formal agreements
- rationale for an acquisition, merger, or strategic alliance
- how injury to competition is being avoided

The regional Bell operating companies, for example, have a tremendous record-keeping burden, between Federal Communications Commission (FCC) regulations and antitrust concerns.

The 1974 AT&T antitrust suit was settled in 1982, when AT&T agreed to divest itself of its 22 local operating companies. Those companies, reorganized into today's seven regional holding companies, and all of their affiliates have continuing obligations and restrictions, including prohibition from entering certain businesses on the grounds that the Baby Bells hold monopoly control over the local exchange. But the regional Bell companies wasted little time in establishing unregulated subsidiaries for business activities outside of their traditional, regulated activities.

Those companies must maintain records showing that the revenues from the regulated side of the business—generated by telephone service customers—are not being used to subsidize any of the unregulated subsidiaries. They also are prohibited from freely sharing information between the regulated and unregulated sides of the business. In 1988, hundreds of employees in one regional telephone company began a formal review of business activities, as required by an agreement with the Department of Justice. A team of lawyers is reviewing thousands of business activities for compliance. Any activities determined not to be within the boundaries of the divestiture agreement must be changed or terminated within 45 days before reporting to the Department of Justice.

OTHER RECORD-KEEPING NECESSITIES

Businesses create and maintain records primarily to meet their internal needs, but laws and government regulations also compel creation of complete and accurate records. Laws and regulations have a greater impact on business today than they did 20 years ago, and they are in a constant state of change. Which of the thousands of federal, state, and local laws and regulations are relevant to a particular business will vary according to:

- the type of business or industry
- how the business is organized
- how and where the company conducts business

The consequences of failure to comply with the law can be serious indeed. Most statutes and regulations stipulate or imply record-keeping requirements, which tend to grow fastest in newly regulated areas and in areas affecting the public welfare or individual rights. Certain records are created and maintained in order to comply with a law or regulation to do so. Other records are created to document a company's compliance with a law or regulation. Record-keeping requirements may include:

- record creation
- a specified form of a record
- record maintenance or preservation
- information reporting or disclosure
- information protection

Mandating good record-keeping are litigation, stricter enforcement of laws, and heavy fines, penalties, and prison sentences. Regulated businesses and those more likely to be involved in litigation will have more extensive record-keeping requirements than other businesses. But any organization may need to make its records available for:

- congressional hearings on a product, service, or business practice
- review, audit, or investigation by government agencies
- civil or criminal proceedings

Accurate record-keeping provides a trail of evidence showing regular patterns of activities to support a company's case. It may lead to a timely, intelligent determination of a safety problem for prompt corrective action and reporting to investigators. Or it may demonstrate the nonexistence of a safety problem or other liability.

Corporate policies and procedures, developed in consultation with legal counsel, also are an important means to compliance with laws and regulations. Policies and their documentation may be especially useful in showing good faith efforts and compliance with various laws.

To avoid violations of software copyright laws, The House of Good Intentions has a corporate policy regarding compliance with software licensing agreements. Audits of software on personal computers are conducted at regular intervals to ensure enforcement of this corporate policy.

A company's records and information management policy and program also contribute to compliance with the law. The legal implications of not having an adequate records program are becoming more serious all the time, and an increasing number of government agencies are requiring a records management program in some form. Records management program documentation may prove beneficial in a court proceeding when the opposing party demands evidence of a formal records management program. (See Chapter 4, "A Day in Court," and Chapter 10, "Records Retention and Disposition," for more on the consequences possible when such evidence is nonexistent.)

A business has an obligation to its shareholders, employees, and other stakeholders to support and defend its claims in civil or criminal proceedings. Proper record-keeping may prevent or minimize the risk of losses in court proceedings or government investigation. When a business does not maintain and protect the right records, the result may be the loss of the right to a proper defense, as discussed in this chapter, or the loss of the right to file a claim, as discussed in the next chapter.

2

Preservation of Legal
Rights and Business Assets

Every business has both a right and a responsibility to protect its legal rights and business assets. As discussed in Chapter 1, a business must maintain and preserve records necessary to defend itself. An organization also will want to create and protect records in order to:

- analyze various business risks
- protect revenues and future income
- reduce or eliminate exposure to risk
- file a claim or prosecute criminal actions

An enterprise relies on its own and others' records and information to analyze, reduce, and eliminate business risks such as new ventures, losses in court proceedings, or a loss of business to a competitor or a disaster. Records also help protect assets and revenues, as well as the legal right to file a claim or to prosecute another party.

CATASTROPHES

The National Fire Protection Association estimates that more than half of the businesses that lose their records in a fire will not survive the next business year. Information-intensive firms that lose computer and other vital records to fire or some other catastrophe may be forced out of business if they have not taken proper precautions.

A fire breaks out in a janitor's closet on the top floor of an office building. All floors suffer some type of damage or loss from heat, smoke, flames, water, and debris. The ForwardThink Corporation's paper files are waterlogged and covered with soot and other debris. Its mainframe computer, which contained customer lists and accounting records, is in need of extensive repair. To resume operations as quickly as possible, ForwardThink leases computer hardware from a local vendor, as per a previously established agreement. Copies of the accounting and customer accounts software and data are recalled from the company's off-site records center for installation on the leased hardware. Damaged paper files are removed to the center for salvage procedures. For their convenience, employees receive a list of affected paper files and the locations of duplicate copies for use in the interim.

Meanwhile, on another floor, the office of Quick 'n' Dirty suffered only minor smoke damage and a power outage. However, most employees are unable to continue their daily activities. The power outage and the tremendous power surge after it was restored caused serious damage to the computer system. Several employees are frantically making calls to find new computer equipment, software, and an army of temporaries to create a new database. The owner has been unable to locate the company's insurance records to determine if there is coverage for disruption of business operations or coverage for the damaged computer equipment.

The potential for a disaster will vary from one location to another. Midwestern businesses will want to consider the odds of damage from a tornado, and coastal companies should consider the same from hurricanes. Urban businesses may have more concern about security against riots and vandalism. Businesses located next to a chemical factory may want to be prepared for a possible fire and explosion that could shut down or engulf their own operations.

A disaster that hits another organization may impact a business when that organization is a major provider of a critical support function or product.

From cut fiber optic cables and power losses to a computer virus or other computer failures, voice and data communications losses have made headlines in recent years. Financial transactions cannot be processed through the Federal Reserve System. Data links are lost between headquarters locations and other facilities or suppliers. Customer inquiries go unanswered.

During one of AT&T's three major long distance services system failures in less than two years, air traffic was backed up nationwide. The infamous Robert T. Morris virus rendered affected computer communications networks useless. A 1988 fire in a telephone switching station outside Chicago caused businesses to shut down for varying lengths of time until communications could be restored. During the first half of 1991, at least three of the regional Bell holding companies experienced computer failures that cut service to millions of business customers in major metro areas and across state lines.

Business continuity plans are becoming a necessity as more businesses experience heavy losses from disaster and as external organizations pressure business to develop such plans. Many government agencies that regulate financial institutions and other industries are requiring a corporate disaster preparedness and recovery plan. Insurance companies may offer breaks in insurance premiums to companies that have a disaster plan.

A disaster plan is much like an insurance policy. One hopes that it never has to be used, but it is there when it is needed. The ultimate purpose of such a plan is to ensure that the business, its employees, and its assets will survive a disastrous event.

The disaster plan of a Charles Schwab & Co. office came to its rescue during the 1989 San Francisco earthquake. The plan identified the airports likely to be open and where to send its computer tapes for processing. The plan also outlined alternatives for phone lines and electronic mail, and where to establish emergency headquarters.

Most organizations have some type of insurance coverage for property damage or loss in the event of a disaster. Some companies also seek coverage for loss of income or expenses while they are closed, or coverage of commissions that must be paid even though the merchandise was destroyed. An organization seeking insurance coverage should ask the following questions:

• What is insurable and what is not?
• What are the extent and limits of coverage?

- How soon after a loss must it be reported?
- What records will be needed to file a claim?

Insurance helps replace buildings and equipment, but it cannot always replace lost information and records. Replacement of lost information may not always be possible, or it may be too expensive. In spite of insurance for the loss of a computer and its software and data, data replacement may not be possible in the absence of appropriate data backup procedures. Insurance for office contents often includes records, but the true value of most records and information cannot be recovered. Insurance cannot replace the loss of proprietary information or the loss of records that preserve a company's rights—including the right to file insurance claims.

Because insurance is not always a quick fix for the loss of records and information, the safeguarding of certain records becomes a major consideration.

One railroad stored thousands of its legal documents that dated back to the nineteenth century in an abandoned bomb shelter. When the area flooded during heavy rains, the ink signatures were washed away from litigation, mineral rights, and right-of-way documents, destroying their estimated value of millions of dollars. The corporation may discover that it has lost certain legal rights in future legal actions that require any of these documents when a question of trustworthiness arises.

In addition to the loss of legal documents, an organization may suffer business and income losses along with its destroyed customer and receivables files and financial and asset records. Records vital to specific industries may include:

- manufacturers' production engineering drawings and specifications
- hospital and clinic patient files
- depositor and investment account records of banks and other financial institutions
- a magazine publisher's subscriber list

Certain records will be required in order to file insurance claims for liability, relocation expenses, business interruption, and other insured expenses and losses. Replacement of insured property may be jeopardized when proof of ownership was destroyed along with the property. Among the first records necessary for the long road to recovery after a catastrophe may be:

- proof of ownership and value of assets that were destroyed
- insurance policies, claim forms, and complete records of premium payments
- profit and expense, and other financial records

Chapter 9, "Records Vital to a Business," includes more information on protection of records from a disaster.

COMPUTER DISASTERS AND COMPUTER CRIMES

A business that depends on data processing and communications will want to protect itself from:

- catastrophes
- electrical power problems
- computer crimes and viruses

As illustrated earlier in this chapter in a scenario about a fire, one company was more prepared than the other for a computer disaster. Other potential computer disasters are operator error, system malfunctions, and power supply problems.

Backup and uninterruptible power systems (UPS) may be installed to prevent data losses and disrupted operations when power to a computer is cut. Power conditioning also is important because the long-term effects of brownouts, power spikes, and line noise have been shown to cause more damage than a major power failure.

Florida is notorious for its severe thunderstorms. During one of those storms, a business reported that its UPS came to its rescue 34 times in one hour.

There are crimes by computer, in which the computer is the criminal's tool, and there are computer crimes, in which the computer is the target of the crime. Experts in high-tech crime can only estimate that the annual costs of unauthorized computer access is $5 billion and growing.

The estimated annual loss of revenues for cellular phone carriers from alteration of equipment and computer records is $200 million. Industry analysts estimate that the clean-up costs alone for the Robert T. Morris virus were about $100 million. Investigation of a break-in to one telephone network involved 42 investigators and a cost of $1.5 million to track the intruder before the company called in the Secret Service.

Illegal access to computers involves committing a crime by altering data or obtaining information for use in a crime. A violator may be a disgruntled employee, an industrial spy, or an embezzler. Long distance and cellular phone service carriers are most vulnerable in recent years to theft of services by computer.

One computer consultant faced charges of computer fraud, interstate transportation of stolen property, and wire fraud. He had obtained AT&T software that collects I.D. codes and passwords of legitimate system users, and he transmitted the software to his friends.

Deterrents to criminal activity and preservation of the means to prosecute such activity may be achieved through computer security policies and procedures for computer networks and desktop and mainframe computer systems. In the words of one law enforcement official on computer hackers: "Cracking a password to get into a system is the same as kicking in a locked door. But when a door is left open, the law may treat the trespasser differently."

REVENUES-EARNING INTELLECTUAL PROPERTIES

Fired by heavy losses worldwide and by increasingly complex technologies, intellectual property protection is moving up on the list of work handled by corporate law firms. They are conducting more intellectual property audits and providing more counseling. Intellectual property litigation cases in the United States have quadrupled in the past 20 years. The U.S. International Trade Commission can halt importation of products that violate American patent laws, but lost profits to overseas sales are more difficult to fight. Hardest hit by the theft of ideas and inventions in the international market are the entertainment, computer software, and pharmaceutical industries.

The federal government can only estimate that counterfeit and fraudulent use of intellectual properties and trademarks costs U.S. business as much as $61 billion each year. The true value of certain information cannot always be determined, and information losses are not always reported outside of an organization.

The costs of shoplifting and employee theft are more easily measured, and the figures tell a compelling story. Shoplifting by strangers costs business $10 billion annually, while theft by employees costs $40 billion each year. Applying this ratio to business information assets, employees are more dangerous threats because, as insiders, they have access to valuable corporate information. Disgruntled and former employees pose an even greater information security risk.

A scientist was apprehended when he attempted to sell trade secrets of a former employer for $10 million. The trade secrets were the formulas and laboratory organisms needed to produce two new drugs. The pharmaceutical company had spent hundreds of millions of dollars to develop each drug. If the scientist had not been caught and convicted, the company's annual sales of $650 million—and growing—would have been severely curtailed, and it might not have been able to recover even its development costs.

A company works too hard to have its best ideas sold or stolen for the quick and easy profits of a thieving competitor. Millions of dollars and years of effort invested in product development could be lost when technical information falls into the hands of a competitor.

The Pharmaceutical Manufacturers Association estimates that the process to introduce a new drug in the United States takes 12 years and costs more than $200 million. When a competitor is able to bring a drug to market before or soon after its developer, without having to invest in research and development, the original developer faces a tough litigation battle while watching hard-earned revenues go into another's pocket.

Efforts to protect intellectual properties are just good business sense. In addition to the loss of property and future revenues, failure to take adequate precautions to guard a trade secret also may result in the loss of the right to protection under the law.

The Quick 'n' Dirty Company discovered that a competitor was contacting its customers and offering the competitor's products at just below its own prices. Furious that the competitor had stolen its customer and pricing lists, considered to be trade secrets, Quick 'n' Dirty sought legal counsel.

Upon review of the situation, the attorney advised against pursuing the case because the firm had not taken measures to protect any of its trade secrets or to prevent disclosure of its customer and pricing information. To make matters worse, the attorney found in records of a recent promotional literature mailing that the competitor was listed as a potential customer. The promotional literature sent to the competitor included not only prices, but a list of Quick 'n' Dirty's "satisfied customers."

Even when a business has properly filed for patent protection of a product or invention, the company may be called upon to defend its patent rights. Patent documentation, such as notarized notes and sketches of concepts in their development, is critical in the costly and time-consuming defense against any patent challenge.

Patent disputes may continue for a number of years, and the legal fees may mount to tens of thousands or even millions of dollars, wiping out any potential profits from the patented products. Critics of a trend in patent disputes today claim that a business with the most litigation clout and staying power can essentially litigate competitors into early settlement or bankruptcy in order to obtain rights to a product.

One small company that depended on two successful products was in the process of implementing a major expansion plan. A temporary injunction was filed by another firm to stop producing one of its products until a pending patent infringement suit was settled. Without the sales from that product, the company was forced to halt its expansion, default on debts, lay off workers, and face large legal expenses.

Software developers turn to copyright and patent law, licensing agreements, and written contracts to protect their investments. The personal computer software industry estimates that nearly $3 billion is lost each year to illegal software copying in the United States and $5.3 billion in Europe. An additional several billion dollars are lost in other markets. The Software Publishers Association, a trade group, is on a campaign to reduce software piracy by writing cease and desist letters and filing piracy lawsuits on behalf of software publishers.

One university's software applications training center was charged with making unauthorized copies of programs and training manuals. In this first suit against a public university, the university agreed to pay $130,000 to the Software Publishers Association and to host a national conference on copyright law and software use.

In another pursuit of violators, two federal marshals and ten lawyers raided one Chicago office. After three hours of examining 125 personal computers, they found enough illegal copies of software that the company paid $300,000 to settle the issue with the software makers.

Corporations also are losing revenues to makers of counterfeit clothing and other merchandise imprinted with corporate logos and copyrighted images. Playing a role in the crackdown on this misuse of intellectual properties are law enforcement agencies, the violated corporations, and even companies specializing in the pursuit of illegal goods and counterfeiters.

The efforts of federal authorities, local police, and 25 different companies resulted in a two-day property seizure of illegal merchandise. Confiscated were 350,000 garments valued at $3 million, and felony indictments are expected.

Not every company takes action against such copyright and trademark violations. Some believe that counterfeiting is as big as the legitimate industry. For example, the popularity of the Teenage Mutant Ninja Turtles sparked an illegal market equal to the legitimate $1 billion merchandise market. With such pervasive violations and the risk of bad press, litigation may not be lucrative for every business.

Headline-making charges of trademark violations in recent years include Saks Fifth Avenue versus Sack's Thrift Avenue, and charges by Eveready against Adolph Coors and other advertisers for use of the Energizer Bunny in their television commercials.

The Walt Disney Company estimates that illegal Disney merchandise generates $1 billion each year for counterfeiters. Employing several attorneys who are dedicated to filing copyright infringement lawsuits, Disney estimates that 25 percent of its 800 lawsuits and regulatory cases handled each year are related to copyright and trademark.

Businesses like Walt Disney seek protection of their profits and corporate image under copyright and trademark laws and licensing agreements. Copyright registration is made through the U.S. Copyright Office, and trademark registration is made through the U.S Patent and Trademark office. Once intellectual properties are registered, an organization may license their use by others.

To retain rights to protection under trademark law, a business must:

- file a use statement within a designated time period of its use
- use the trademark consistently and continuously
- report trademark infringements
- file protests against any similar mark in a pending patent application
- file affidavits during the sixth year after registration
- register ownership changes
- renew the registration during the twentieth year of its use

Chapter 8, "Records and Information Security," provides additional information on applications of the law and other tactics for protection of intellectual properties.

Competitor Intelligence and Industrial Espionage

International business travelers are experiencing a fear of spies that is surpassing the fear of terrorism. U.S. officials report that several foreign intelligence services are using their vast resources to collect economic information instead of military secrets in an economic world war. The French Secret Service was recently exposed for its industrial espionage campaign. Government officials note that France is not the only foreign country spying on U.S. businesses—it is the only one that was caught.

Estimated losses are in the hundreds of millions of dollars in three headline-making cases of U.S. companies located in France. Government intelligence services, pitching patriotism, had recruited nationals to work for U.S. subsidiaries as corporate spies. French employees of IBM and Texas Instruments reportedly handed over company documents to French intelligence agents, who then passed them on to a French computer maker. In another case, hotel maids, who actually worked for intelligence, copied bid documents that were eventually given to government-owned Air France.

Executives traveling abroad are advised to fly commercial carriers and to make their reservations at the last minute so that surveillance arrangements cannot be easily made. They are cautioned about the possibility of hidden microphones and undercover flight attendants and hotel maids. Executives must keep a tight grip on sensitive documents to prevent a search of briefcases and luggage for:

- marketing strategies and business plans
- research data
- technical specifications
- bid data

Several foreign intelligence services are intercepting overseas communications of U.S. companies by capturing satellite signals or picking up transmissions passing through government-owned telephone exchanges.

After examining patterns of competitive bids that were coming in too close on its overseas bids, Caterpillar, Inc. is now putting most of its overseas communications into code. General Electric's jet engine division is scrambling its phone conversations and fax transmissions.

Various methods of gathering information about other businesses are legal, and some are not. There are other tactics that may be questioned on ethical grounds. Competitor intelligence gathering may be based on overt and covert tactics. Measuring the amount of rust on a train track to determine the volume of shipments into and out of a plant is one of the more covert tactics used in the past. Additional covert tactics are:

- surveillance and bugging
- unauthorized computer access
- extortion or blackmail
- theft
- dumpster diving

Dumpster diving for documents has been declared legal by the U.S. Supreme Court. Once trash is at a curb or in another container where it is open to scavengers, the owner can no longer have an expectation of privacy.

One company discovered that its unshredded customer charge account information had been pulled from its trash dumpster so that the information could be used to make illegitimate purchases on those accounts. Another company's 1/4-inch shredded drafts, duplicate copies, and rejected photocopies had been painstakingly pieced together by a competitor, who consistently was beating out the company on price in bid proposals.

In another situation, a private security guard witnessed two men pick up the trash outside an executive's home. The guard followed the men to a foreign consulate building. In response to a government inquiry, the consulate explained that it was looking for grass cuttings to fill a hole, which had been dug for a pool that now could not be completed. Officials suspect that they were really after discarded documents containing valuable information that might be of use to businesses in that country.

Mountains of valuable competitive information can be gathered without resorting to cloak and dagger tactics. Membership in the Society of Competitor Intelligence Professionals was up to more than 1,700 in 1990. The society estimates that the top 60 corporate users of corporate intelligence services spend more than $30 million a year to get that information. *Fortune* magazine reports that 80 percent of the Fortune 1,000 employ personnel as competitive analysts for intelligence-gathering activities.

Market research firms and competitive analysts—of the ethical variety—rely on public information to do their jobs. Their sources include:

- direct contact with knowledgeable individuals
- published and unpublished public records and government information
- corporate public relations packets
- trade shows
- computerized information database services
- disassembly or chemical analysis of a rival's product

Information Disclosure Rights and Responsibilities

Occasionally, a business is required to disclose information to an outside party. Certain government and legal demands for information disclosure may place that information into the hands of others or into the public domain:

- subpoena and the discovery process in litigation
- court proceedings and government investigations
- government agency reporting and disclosure requirements
- state reporting and disclosure requirements

There are situations in which it may be appropriate and desirable to reveal trade secrets to another party, such as in a joint venture or when contracting for products and services.

The TechTrack firm is developing a peripheral to be marketed in conjunction with a personal computer system. Both TechTrack and the computer manufacturer must share proprietary information and other trade secrets, such as marketing plans, so that the peripheral's design will be compatible with the computer system. To ensure the appropriate use of the information and to prevent disclosure beyond the joint partnership, both companies sign nondisclosure agreements, and they carefully mark valuable and sensitive information for easy identification by both parties.

There are a few owners of proprietary information who are reluctant to do business with the federal government because of its voluminous specifications and its information disclosure requirements.

One maker of a new metal alloy for use in aircraft will not do business with the Pentagon so that it can avoid having to reveal its technical data and production costs. A microchip producer also foregoes government business because it believes the stringent testing requirements actually render its product less dependable than originally designed.

When doing business with the government, a company must consider if the information disclosure to the agency will be subject to the Freedom of Information Act (FOIA). With certain exceptions, the public has a right to request valuable business data that is on file with federal agencies. Unless specific information falls into an exemption category, a company may seek to block the release of proprietary information through a reverse-FOIA lawsuit. Exempted categories of information include:

- classified documents related to national defense and foreign policy
- information exempt under other laws, such as income tax returns

- confidential business information, such as trade secrets or commercial and financial data
- personal or private information, such as employee and medical files

See Chapter 8, "Records and Information Security," for more on information releases to others.

COLLECTION OF RECEIVABLES AND OTHER MONIES DUE

A company may suffer business and financial losses from legal actions or the inability to collect monies due when certain records are prematurely destroyed:

- customer and receivables records
- sales agreements and purchasing contracts
- other contracts

Contracts and sales agreements spell out the rights and responsibilities of two or more parties. Those documents and the records documenting related activities and events may become critical when a business has difficulty collecting funds owed to the company for its products or services.

The TechTrack firm contracted with a client to provide software and technical manuals for the client's 50 office sites. In the purchase agreement, the client agreed to pay for the software and manuals within 30 days after installation of the software. After months of telephone calls and past-due invoices, TechTrack decided to initiate legal proceedings to collect on the account. The contract, installation schedule, and the acceptance documents signed by staff in each client location were used to show that the TechTrack firm had satisfactorily fulfilled its contractual obligations and that the client owed the money due, plus finance charges and legal fees.

Agreements and other documentation also may be required when an organization chooses to file a claim against another party for failure to perform as specified in a contract.

The House of Good Intentions contracted out renovation work on one of its facilities. Careless contract employees caused extensive damage to existing carpeting and finished wood trim, and they demolished a sculpture valued at $100,000. The contract stipulated that the contractor would be liable for any property damage that occurred as a result of its actions. The House of Good Intentions had records documenting the value of the damaged sculpture and other furnishings, and the contractor eventually paid The House of Good Intentions $200,000 to cover the losses.

Certain business records must be maintained for long periods of time to continue protecting a company's rights and future income. Records dating back to the 1800's that declare mineral rights and right-of-ways hold significant value today for railroads and other businesses.

A private marine-exploration company discovered the largest sunken treasure in American history: thousands of mint-condition gold coins and rare gold bars valued at up to $1 billion. The treasure was found in a ship that sank more than a century ago. A U.S. district judge rejected the arguments of eight insurance companies that were attempting to stake a claim to the treasure, ruling that the exploration group can keep the treasure.

The judge determined that the insurance companies had intentionally abandoned their rights to any recovery when they destroyed the records related to the ship's demise. The companies had kept no copies of insurance policies, invoices for shipments, or other records to establish a claim for the gold. Nor had they attempted to recover the ship. The insurance companies argued that they had paid out claims arising from the disaster, but the only existing documentation of that fact were newspaper accounts that contained too many discrepancies to be considered reliable proof. (An appeal is pending at the time of this writing.)

The longer records are to be maintained, the more likely the need for special measures to preserve the documents.

The ForwardThink Corporation has a number of property deeds dated from 1920 to 1940. Those documents may be required to prove land ownership well into the next century. Because of the extremely poor quality of paper produced in the first half of this century, ForwardThink has microfilmed the deeds and de-acidified the paper documents. The original and microfilmed deeds are stored in separate facilities with environmental and security controls.

CRIMINAL ACTIONS

The magnitude of information crimes and security breaches is difficult to document because most crimes go unreported. Many businesses attempt to resolve the problem internally in order to avoid any embarrassment, inconvenience, and possible damage from a public trial.

White-collar crime is often dependent upon a company's records and information. Highly competitive industries are more vulnerable to white-collar crime than other industries. Risks of embezzlement, misappropriation of trade secrets, and misuse of computers also tend to increase in hard economic times.

White-collar crime is more widespread and uncontrolled today than it was 20 years ago. New technologies are making it easier for disgruntled employees, greedy competitors, and adventurous computer hackers to violate information security measures. Documents can easily be forged or altered using laser printers and high-quality photocopiers. Digitized information can be deleted, modified, or sent without detection through far-reaching computer networks.

A business has a responsibility to its stakeholders to protect itself from undue harm caused by unlawful activities. Concerns about a damaged reputation when a reported crime hits the news may go by the wayside when stockholders or others clamor to hold someone accountable for criminal actions that cause severe harm to a business, its employees or customers, or the general public.

Information security policies and procedures help protect an organization from information security crimes and crimes committed as a result of information security breaches. Documentation of those policies and practices helps preserve the right to prosecute criminal actions and attempt to obtain restitution.

The House of Good Intentions has a clearly stated information security policy and set of procedures to identify and protect its sensitive and valuable records and information. It also has established an incident response team, composed of an investigator, legal advisor, computer specialist, auditor, and public relations manager. The team is trained in company information policy and basic investigative techniques so that it is able to collect and properly handle any evidence that may be necessary to file charges against or impose sanctions on the offending party. The team determines what steps are necessary to minimize damages and to prevent future violations of a similar nature.

Guidelines are needed for what to do in the event of an information security breach. Without careful thought to this issue, there may be a public relations disaster or possible violations of the law if efforts to identify a mole are too aggressive.

In 1991, Procter & Gamble Co. received mixed reviews of its actions to identify information leaks within the company. Based on a state statute that makes it illegal to disclose business secrets outside of the employing company, Procter & Gamble persuaded law enforcement authorities to use telephone records to track news leaks from employees to the *Wall Street Journal*. Some applauded the company for finding a new way to discover leaks. Others were critical of the approach or skeptical about the constitutionality of the state law, claiming that any statute making it a crime to speak may be unconstitutional based on the First Amendment. An additional criticism was that the state law used does not specify what is confidential business information.

Most state laws have loose definitions of what constitutes a business or trade secret, so business must assume the responsibility to define this. Employees, business partners, suppliers, and others must be given fair warning about what may be a criminal activity.

The information or idea must be worth protecting in the first place because it gives an advantage to its owner over those who do not have the information. The information owner must take appropriate measures to prevent the secret from becoming available to others without prior authorization. Key documentation that may become necessary to prosecute trade secret law violations includes:

- confidentiality agreements with employees, suppliers, and others
- records of employee training sessions on information security
- documentation of information security policies and practices

Chapter 8, "Records and Information Security," provides more detail on records protection and preservation of rights to take action against a criminal.

3

Employer Rights and Responsibilities

Personnel costs are the single greatest expense for most businesses. These costs include salaries, benefits, taxes, training, and turnover. There also are costs in the forms of:

* litigation
* compliance with laws and government regulations
* employee threats to intellectual properties and information security

Employee record-keeping is necessary for business management planning and decision-making. Records preserve the many details to be remembered year after year for a changing number of workers. Keeping accurate employee records also is a good business practice that meets the various government requirements and protects a business.

Employers have a number of rights and responsibilities regarding their workers relating to personnel actions, health, safety, payment of wages and taxes, privacy, protection of intellectual property, and more. Records are created, reported, maintained, and protected in order to comply with government record-keeping requirements or to show that the business is in compliance with employment laws and regulations. Records also are created, maintained, and protected in order to preserve certain rights of the employer:

* the right to a proper defense

- the right to file a claim against another party
- the right to protect assets of the business

EMPLOYERS ON THE DEFENSE

Not every business is affected by all federal employment laws, but an employer may be subject to the requirements of every state in which it has employees. State laws tend to pattern themselves after federal laws, and they usually extend their impact to companies smaller than those affected by federal laws.

The intent of employment law is to protect the innocent worker. Regulatory agencies, legislation, and the courts are taking over the historical role of organized labor to protect the worker as we move from an industrial to a service economy. But employment law has become a measurable threat to even the fairest and most generous employer.

Claims and charges by employees and government agencies have become an inevitable part of doing business in today's regulated and litigating business environment. Economic downturns, sympathetic juries, and media hype contribute to increasing employment litigation risks for employers. The risk of being sued rises each time a court defines what constitutes unfair, unethical, or discriminatory behavior.

Most businesses are eager to settle employee claims out of court, because of the:

- expenses involved in defending themselves
- potential of a damaged reputation
- risks of additional similar suits
- tendency of juries to be sympathetic to workers

Employment laws and regulations directly or indirectly influence personnel record-keeping practices. A number of them stipulate that a business must create, collect, and maintain or report certain records. Reporting or information disclosure requirements by government agencies cover payroll, benefits, taxes, equal employment opportunity, safety, health, and other functions or activities.

Other laws compel the creation of records in order to show compliance with a law. It is in the best interest of a business to collect and maintain accurate and complete records that demonstrate compliance with an employment law, even if the law has no record-keeping requirements.

Good record-keeping practices help prepare for litigation and government investigation or audit, by documenting compliance with the law to minimize the risks and losses. Complete, accurate, and indisputable records may deter an employee or agency from even filing charges. Or such records may encourage an employee to drop unfounded charges, or to settle out of court.

When a company becomes the target of an investigation and has not created and maintained records according to a government requirement, it could have serious difficulties defending itself and may be subject to fines and penalties.

Under the Immigration Act, every employer must verify that all persons who are hired after November, 1986 are eligible to work in the United States. The employer must document that verification on the Employment Eligibility Verification form, or the I-9 form. Each I-9 form must be retained for three years from the date the employee is hired, or for one year past the employee's termination, whichever is longer. The penalty for not properly completing, retaining, or presenting an I-9 form for inspection by government officials is a fine from $100 to $1,000 for each violation. Penalties for knowingly creating, using, or accepting fraudulent documents to verify identity and employment eligibility are fines from $250 to $2,000 for each fraudulent document and for every incidence of its use, creation, or acceptance.

The Department of Labor, the Equal Employment Opportunity Commission (EEOC), and the IRS are among a number of different agencies that rely on records showing proper payment of wages, taxes, and other employee payments. When a question arises regarding payment of minimum wage or taxes, overtime practices, discrimination in pay or benefits, and other claims, the following records may be among those reviewed:

- wages, overtime, sales commission payments
- other employee payments (bonuses, perks, educational assistance)
- income tax withholdings
- unemployment taxes
- worker compensation payments
- Social Security taxes

- health benefit plans and payments
- retirement and pension plans and payments
- death benefits

Business uses of independent contractors over the years have been for staffing flexibility, reduced costs, and other reasons. But IRS reviews one year resulted in reclassification of 76,000 workers from independent contractor to employee and proposed tax assessments of close to $100 million. The waters remain murky about what constitutes an independent contractor, in spite of the IRS's 20 questions to help determine a distinction.

To defend itself in an IRS review, a business should consider documentation of practices that respond to the IRS criteria for independent contractors, including records of scheduling, hours worked, training, location of work, etc. A record of the prevalent worker classification practices of other companies in the industry also may be helpful. If the IRS determines that contractors are employees, a business may need to cough up back taxes, interest, and penalties for all workers in the position reviewed. It also may be vulnerable to liabilities in any claims filed by the employee(s) for benefits.

Safety and Health

Inadequate and inaccurate records are especially harmful on matters regarding worker health and safety issues. Prosecutors are bringing more criminal charges, and executives are receiving jail sentences for reckless endangerment of lives. Efforts to meet compliance with health and safety regulations must be shown in court or in government inspections, audits, or investigations.

OSHA found 221 violations at one manufacturing plant. Of the 130 willful violations, 129 involved faulty record-keeping. The penalties assessed against the plant totaled $1.4 million, of which the charges for poor record-keeping were $1.29 million. The case was then turned over for criminal prosecution.

Safety program records that may help provide evidence of compliance include:

- risk management and safety program documentation

- company policies, procedures, and standards to eliminate or reduce hazardous practices and conditions
- employee education and training activities
- vehicle maintenance and accident reports
- employee accident and illness reports
- medical files and benefits payments
- short-term and long-term disability records

The workplace safety issue of the nineties is ergonomics. Its impact goes beyond manufacturing environments to even the smallest of office sites.

One manufacturer was hit with a $1.6 million fine for alleged flagrant violations of workplace safety regulations at its plant. After on-site inspections, OSHA cited the corporation for 264 violations, all but two of which were considered serious. OSHA reported that work conditions resulted in repetitive motion disorders requiring 300 employees to seek medical help, of whom 25 underwent surgical procedures. Among the charges were 100 record-keeping violations, each assessed a fine of $2,000. The corporation had improperly recorded, or failed to record, the cumulative trauma disorders as required on an OSHA log of injuries and illnesses.

Another health and safety issue is drugs and the workplace. Fearing liabilities of intoxicated workers, businesses are restricting alcohol consumption at company-sponsored events and off-premises client entertainment. Documented policies against alcohol mixed with client entertainment—including a policy not to reimburse travel and entertainment expenses for alcohol—help show a company's commitment to safety. Federal contractors and major employers also must ensure a drug-free workplace.

Records are needed to show that a drug-free workplace policy has been established and to show good-faith efforts to enforce the policy. The government may want to see evidence of regular communications regarding the policy, such as seminars, posters, newsletter items, and anti-drug notices enclosed with paychecks. Companies involved in national defense work or transportation must adopt a drug testing program and reporting procedures. A federal contractor must report to the government if an employee is convicted of drug law violations that occurred on the job, and also report the sanctions taken against the worker.

Worker exposure to toxic substances is another high-risk area for employers. In its defense, a business must have records relating to:

* hazardous conditions and substances (air quality tests, records of spills and clean-up operations, etc.)
* efforts to adequately warn employees of the risks and to provide training on proper handling of materials
* actions taken to increase safety
* effects of exposure on workers

State prosecutors increasingly are bringing criminal charges against companies and executives based on state laws that are tougher than federal laws.

A 1984 indictment was the first case in the nation in which employers were criminally charged with aggravated battery for allegedly harming workers by exposing them to toxic chemicals. The long court battle and criminal court trial ended in 1991 when a judge acquitted the five current and former executives accused of endangering the health of workers. The judge ruled that the company had met safety standards set by OSHA, and that prosecutors had not proven that the worker injuries were a result of workplace conditions.

As protective labor laws come under fire for being discriminatory, companies may be exposed to new health and safety liabilities. Fetal protection policies, formerly a bona fide occupational qualification exception allowed as essential to a safe workplace, are now considered a form of sex bias.

A recent U.S. Supreme Court decision prohibits sex discrimination through company policies that prevent women from working in jobs with potential risk to fetuses. In spite of court reassurances otherwise, this decision increases a company's exposure to liability lawsuits. Even when an employer is not negligent, and when it obtains a signed release from liability by the mother, a personal injury suit may still be brought not only by the mother, but years later by any child born with a defect.

Employment Actions

An employer generally cannot foresee when and if a hearing or lawsuit will occur regarding an employment action, but events and practices must be documented, just in case. Good documentation may prove that a hiring or firing decision was valid. Employment actions to be documented include:

- selection for hiring
- pay and other compensation
- selection for promotion, layoff, recall, education and training opportunities, early retirement, and so on.
- performance appraisals
- employee grievances or complaints
- disciplinary action or demotion
- termination

A labor attorney should review a company's policies and procedures regarding employment actions. The attorney also should review any personnel manual, employment contracts, and other employee record-keeping practices. The attorney can advise on what specific records to keep, what records not to keep, and how long those records should be kept. (See also Chapter 10, "Records Retention and Disposition.")

A company's personnel records are used not only in its defense; they also may be used by a plaintiff to support its case against an employer. Judges traditionally grant plaintiffs broad access to defendant records in bias cases because the employer—not the worker—has all the facts and records. Government agencies also may have access to employer books and records for audits and investigations.

A paper trail of evidence to back up a company's reasoning and actions may be necessary one day. The key to avoiding problems and reducing risks is to begin record-keeping efforts at the inception of employment and continue them through termination:

- hiring phase documentation
- documentation throughout employment to show that employee policies and procedures were applied consistently and equitably
- documentation of termination process

Records of employee performance and employment actions should be created consistently and on a regular basis for all employees. Documentation of events should be direct observations (not hearsay) and should be completed in a timely manner, as close as possible to the time of their occurrence. Both positive and negative job-related performance should be recorded. All documentation should be accurate and factual. (At the time of this writing, the Supreme Court is considering whether to hear a case that could define the extent to which companies can be sued for libel, based on personnel-file memos written by supervisors.)

Because a complaint of discrimination may be filed within 180 days of an action, records of an employment action must be maintained for this time period to defend against any discrimination charges. They may be retained longer for other purposes, as discussed later in Chapter 10, "Records Retention and Disposition."

The Department of Labor and individual state labor departments sometimes broaden a complaint review to include additional employees. They also may conduct a review without a complaint having been filed.

ForwardThink Corporation receives a letter from the EEOC indicating that the company has been selected for a compliance review. The letter requests that a copy of the company's affirmative action program and supporting data be sent within 30 days. The vice president of human resources collects copies of its affirmative action policy statement and affirmative action programs specific to protected classes of workers. Also pulled are data related to workforce makeup and employment actions. After the documentation review, the EEOC will conduct an on-site visit to review additional data and to interview selected employees. If the EEOC's final data analysis finds no significant deviation, no other evidence will be required. If there appears to be a problem, the chief executive of ForwardThink will be informed of the allegations of discrimination.

Evidence that may be necessary to refute allegations of discrimination include:

- job group profiles
- job placement files (job requisition, advertising copy, job candidate files, documentation of the review and selection process, documentation of any testing, etc.)
- guidelines, reports, and analyses on compensation and salary plans

- selection processes used and a history of employee transfers, layoffs, promotions, educational and training opportunities, etc.

In addition to documentation of how existing policies and practices were followed, a business must be able to articulate a legitimate business reason for when those policies and practices were not binding in a particular instance. Employment decisions that result in a disparate effect or adverse impact may be allowed under certain circumstances. For example, a small business that cannot afford to modify its delivery truck to accommodate every type of handicapped operator may not be open to charges of discrimination against the handicapped for that particular job function.

The Bureau of National Affairs reported in 1990 that more than 25,000 wrongful discharge suits were pending in state and federal courts. Accurate and timely completion of documentation regarding termination may spare an employer litigation and expense. The more objective and quantifiable the documentation, the better. The employer may need to show that the termination was for business-related reasons, such as poor performance or financial cutbacks, and that no discrimination was involved. Additional records and information considerations regarding terminations include information disclosure requirements, such as notification to the employee of the right to continue health insurance coverage for a limited time, or the Plant Closing Law, which requires advance notice of layoff.

As the workforce ages and as business reduces costs by laying off top managers, age discrimination has become the fastest-growing claim in recent years. At the time of this writing, the Supreme Court is torn between the employer having to present evidence or having to prove that an employment decision that resulted in a discriminatory impact, such as age discrimination, was based solely on financial or other necessary business considerations. If the employer only needs to present evidence, it would then be up to the employee to prove that a nondiscriminatory alternative existed that would still serve the company's business goals.

Documentation becomes even more critical when a termination follows shortly upon any sensitive occurrences, such as an employee claim for worker compensation or a complaint made to a government agency about discrimination, work conditions, or business activities. Such a termination may be construed as retaliation, which is forbidden by law. Any termination found to be in breach of public policy is considered a wrongful discharge.

Also considered wrongful discharge is a termination found to be in breach of contract. The force of the employment-at-will doctrine continues to be eroded by common law and statutes, such as those prohibiting discrimination. Any implied or explicit employment agreements also void the employment-at-will doctrine.

In one major oil company, a homosexual employee had left a personal document on a copy machine that other employees found to be repulsive. The document was a party invitation with the "house rules" for a gay party. The company fired the employee shortly after that incident, in spite of the fact that the employee had a record of exemplary job performance. A California Superior Court judge found that the company had violated assurances that it would not fire any employee except for unsatisfactory job performance, and awarded the terminated employee $5.3 million in damages.

Contracts and Agreements

Contracts and agreements with employees are records to be protected, along with records that document compliance with the terms of the contracts.

Both organized labor contracts and individual employment agreements spell out the rights and obligations of the employer and the employee. Documentation of how the employer is in compliance with the terms and conditions of legally binding documents may eventually be necessary for a proper defense against any claim, or for the business to file a claim against another party.

Most individual employment agreements stipulate the compensation and benefits for performance of designated job duties. Many go beyond that to include other clauses, such as the right of the employer to terminate the employee at any time for cause or in the event of the sale, merger, or discontinuance of the business.

Employers in employment-at-will states may terminate nonunion employees for any reason, as long as there is no discrimination or binding contract. Some companies make use of termination contracts, which release the employer from specified liabilities. However, the Older Workers Benefit Protection Act stipulates that employees should have 45 days to consider a waiver agreement not to sue under age bias law.

Termination in breach of a contract—express or implied—is a primary basis for wrongful discharge claims. Express contracts are those written agreements signed by both the employer and employee. Implied contracts may be verbal agreements, employee handbooks, or other promises made by the employer or employee. Breach of contract violations typically result in payment of back pay and lost benefits. Frequently, damages regarding emotional distress and punitive damages are also awarded.

The rules of business contracts have been applied in certain court cases involving employee contracts.

The House of Good Intentions asked one of its top managers to relocate to another site which was having serious financial difficulties. After only six months, the company closed the site and terminated the employee. The employee took the House of Good Intentions to court based on the fact that the employee was not informed of the serious financial difficulties prior to negotiation of the relocation. The court decided, based on business contract law, that this information should have been disclosed to the employee as information that the plaintiff needed to make a decision about whether to enter into the contract.

Employment contracts and other employee records must be carefully reviewed by legal counsel to minimize the risk of letting a judge or jury interpret its wording. The language of employee handbooks or contracts must be carefully worded to avoid any implied or expressed contracts or promises that the company may not be able to fulfill.

The documentation of policies, procedures, and contracts, as well as documentation of compliance with them, may be critical in the event of government or civil action. An employer may need to show how the employee handbook provisions and policies are applied equally to all employees—especially handbooks that stipulate any procedures for disciplinary and termination actions.

Judges have ruled that employees, as well as employers, can be held to their written statements, as in an employee handbook. If arbitration provisions in a handbook are found to be binding, a fired employee must exhaust the grievance procedures outlined in the handbook before suing in federal court. One judge wrote: "If a plaintiff seeks to rely on provisions in a handbook as the course of an implied contract of employment, then he must accept the agreement as a whole. In short, the plaintiff must accept his obligations along with his rights, as in any agreement."

Worker's Right to Privacy

Issues about employee privacy keep showing up in courts. From reference checks and drug testing to employee surveillance and searches, there are many areas in which an employee can charge a company with invasion of privacy.

Companies with electronic and voice messaging systems are encountering privacy issues. Forwardthink Corporation has a policy that places these systems into the context of office-privacy issues and company records, including telephone calls, contents of desk drawers, correspondence, and other records and information. Voice messaging and electronic mail systems are to be used only for transmission of messages dealing with legitimate business activities. Messages may be intercepted only for designated reasons, such as system maintenance or investigation of possible employee fraud or compromise of confidential company information.

Employers are required by law to inform job applicants when a credit history is being used to evaluate them. The FTC currently is seeking voluntary compliance with the law.

One corporation agreed to settle charges that it failed to tell job applicants that information in their credit reports influenced the decision not to hire them. The FTC said that the employment reports marketed by credit-reporting agencies often contain more information than that in the standard credit reports used by banks and retailers. Under the consent agreement, the corporation is required to mail letters to applicants that were denied jobs because of a credit report, stating the reasons they were not hired and the name and address of the agency that supplied the company with the damaging report. The company must comply with the Federal Fair Credit Reporting Act and maintain documents to prove its compliance for the next five years.

Employee files contain personal information that is protected by privacy and other laws or regulations. A number of federal and state privacy laws exist to protect the individual by controlling the collection, maintenance, access, use, and dissemination of personal information. Summary personnel records that do not identify individuals are created most frequently for management purposes and to show overall compliance with laws and regulations, as discussed earlier in this chapter. Records specific to an individual employee typically include:

- personal data
- employment history
- wage and salary data
- attendance records
- performance appraisals
- payroll information (payments, deductions)
- tax payments
- benefits program records
- health and accident reports
- skills inventories
- training and education programs completed
- corporate training and communications activities on discrimination, harassment, drug-free workplace, and so forth.
- employment actions

In general, the right to access employee records belongs to the employee, the government, law enforcement authorities, and company employees with a legitimate need to know. State laws may specify the types of records for review and any allowed exclusions. Collective bargaining agreements may provide guidelines for access to employee information. A business is subject to criminal penalties for any damages that may occur as a result of a willful or intentional action that violates privacy rights.

ForwardThink Corporation has a corporate policy on employee records. This policy states that the individual employee and others with a business need to access employee information may access that employee's records. (Those with a legitimate need to know include payroll and human resources staff, an employee's supervisor, and management personnel.) The policy goes on to state that individuals have the right to know what records are maintained about them and who has access to these records. Employees may submit written requests to review their records (to ensure retrieval of the proper record) and may request amendment to those records to correct any errors. Procedures are established for adequate safeguards to prevent unauthorized disclosure or misuse of the information, and to maintain an accounting of information disclosure made beyond those in the performance of normal business activities, such as to law enforcement authorities.

More information on safeguarding employee records is provided in Chapter 8, "Records and Information Security."

THE EMPLOYER'S RIGHT TO PROTECT ASSETS

An employer's right to protect its assets includes the right to expect employee compliance with the company's intellectual properties and records management practices. Policies, procedures, and formal agreements help protect these rights.

A clause in an employment contract may address confidentiality issues and protection of an organization's intellectual properties. When confidentiality or noncompetition is important enough in an organization, those issues may be treated in a separate employment agreement. The contract also may stipulate injunctive relief or legal damages for breach of any of the contract's provisions.

Typically, employment contracts or agreements formally assign to the employer the rights to inventions, writings, and other products that are developed in the course of employment. There also may be a "loyalty and due care" clause in a contract, prohibiting any personal actions that would be in conflict with the company's interest and any unlawful or negligent acts. If the likelihood of mistakes through human error is significant, an organization may include standards of best efforts or good faith.

The laws across the country differ regarding unfair competition, including solicitation of employees or clients by a worker before leaving an employer. A carefully worded restrictive covenant, or noncompete agreement, may protect an employer from such actions. In one case, both the violating employee and the hiring organization were found to have engaged in unfair trade practices.

A salesman had a contract with ForwardThink Corporation that barred him from joining a competitor within 12 months of leaving ForwardThink Corporation. A rival corporation hired the employee, promising to pay the employee's legal fees if he were to be sued by the former employer. ForwardThink did sue, and a jury awarded the firm $12,000 in damages for breach of contract plus $100,000 in punitive damages. The jury also hit the new employer with $15,000 in damages for unfair trade practices because of its promise to pay the employee's legal fees. The judge awarded $250,000 to ForwardThink for attorney fees.

Another example would be protection from employees leaving a business to start their own competing business.

The owner of one small advertising agency walked into the office one morning to discover resignation letters of four top employees. They had moved out in the middle of the night to start their own business, taking computer equipment, files, supplies, and more than $35,000 worth of client artwork. The owner is charging the four employees with the loss of $250,000 in accounts and business, theft of trade secrets and property, and failure to devote their time to the agency's business interests in the last few months of employment.

Employment contracts may restate, and clarify, the common law requirements that employees not divulge or wrongfully use a company's trade secrets. An employee in violation of trade secret laws may be liable to the employer for damages stemming from lost profits and for punitive damages. An employment agreement also may clearly state that the employee must comply with company policies and practices, including record-keeping and information security practices.

The employer has certain responsibilities to protect these rights. An organization should develop and enforce company policy, including a policy against records and computers in the workplace that are personal property. (Under the Communications Privacy Act, the company may be prohibited from auditing any corporate data that is stored on such a system.)

Without appropriate employee education on record-keeping and information security policies and practices, the employer will not be able to hold the employee accountable for compliance with those policies and procedures. Employees must be trained on:

- what records are to be protected
- how they are to be protected
- restrictions on copying or removing company records, files, and documents
- the proper handling and destruction of sensitive and valuable records

When an employee is terminated, for whatever reason, a procedure must be in place that ensures the collection of all proprietary information in documents, manuals, and other company records that may be in the possession of the employee.

When it comes to white-collar crime by employees, prevention has been more effective than attempts to obtain restitution. Useful preventive measures include:

- employee background checks
- company standards of conduct
- security plans
- methods to remove temptation and opportunity

To prepare for information security violations, an organization will determine procedures to be followed in the event of security breaches and any sanctions for violation of security procedures. When a violation occurs, an incident response team may determine what steps are necessary to minimize the damages and to prevent further violations of a similar nature. This team—including an investigator, legal advisor, computer specialist, and auditor—should be trained in company information policy and basic investigative techniques in order to be able to collect and properly handle evidence that will be necessary to file any charges or claims against the offending party.

Any organizational change that affects the job status of individual employees—such as a merger, downsizing, or relocation—may create conditions ripe for employee sabotage and other threats to its records and information. Information security should become a higher priority during such times to guard against threats from disgruntled employees. An organization must pay more attention to accurate, comprehensive record-keeping in order to be prepared for the greater potential for litigation or investigation resulting from the organizational changes.

See Chapters 7 and 8 for more on employee threats to information security and on information security practices.

Personal Records

Any record created by an employee that documents activities performed within the scope of employment or that uses company resources would be considered a company record. There should be a company policy and employee training regarding what is a business record and the fact that such records are subject to the review and control of the organization, including:

- calendars with itineraries
- notations of expenses to be claimed as deductions by the company
- meetings schedules and notes
- managers' files on employees
- electronic or voice messaging systems

Employees tend to set up their own records systems for a number of reasons. Most often it is because an employee lacks confidence in the company's records system, or the employee simply wants the convenience of having records close at hand. Occasionally an employee creates and maintains records separately from standard business records for a self-serving purpose. Some employees simply find it difficult to throw out anything.

The TechTrack firm, wanting tight control over its highly confidential documents, established a standard procedure for certain documents to be destroyed by the recipient after they were read. But one employee made photocopies of those documents before their destruction. Discovering this violation of policy too late, TechTrack saw those documents eventually surface again and be used against the firm in a lawsuit.

Very serious problems may develop when employees are allowed to have personal records separate from official company records. Costly record-keeping inefficiencies are only one consideration. Because individuals destroy these records only when they see fit, and not according to the company's record retention schedule, such action may be considered selective destruction. Any evidence of selective destruction may jeopardize the integrity of the company's record retention program. (See Chapter 10, "Records Retention and Disposition.")

Another difficulty with personal records is how they are treated in the event of litigation or investigation. Because such records are not created in the normal course of business, there is no documentation of the procedures for their creation and maintenance. As such, they may not be considered trustworthy enough as evidence in a company's defense. However, they are subject to subpoena by an adverse party and would be considered an admission of the creating organization, the employer.

The House of Good Intentions initiated company training sessions on discrimination in the workplace that required managers to confront their own biases in order to correct the problems. When a group of minority and female employees later sued the company for discrimination, plaintiff attorneys were overjoyed during pretrial discovery to review the records from those training sessions. Employee comments and handwritten notes from various training exercises were used to show that discriminatory attitudes did in fact exist throughout the company. The House of Good Intentions argued against use of the notes in court because the remarks—taken out of context—were given not as opinions, but as examples of stereotypes. The judge ruled that the workshop notes could be used as evidence against the firm. Facing the difficult task of arguing that the notes do not really mean what they say, the House of Good Intentions is considering settlement of the lawsuit, in spite of the fact that it claims it is innocent of the discrimination charges.

A number of cases appearing in the news over the past few years have involved current and former employees who maintained their own records system. Employees have created or maintained records to document mistakes by other employees or in anticipation of filing a wrongful discharge claim. In another situation, records that should have been destroyed according to the company's record retention schedule were removed by an employee and stored in the basement of his home. Eventually, those records wound up in a government investigation that showed price-fixing on the part of the company.

In short, personal records usually do not help a company, and they may in fact prove to be harmful. A records management program must have control over the creation and management of all business records, including those in employees' offices and desks. (See Chapter 10, "Records Retention and Disposition," for more information on maintaining the integrity of a record retention and destruction program.) Note, however, that legal counsel must be involved in the determination of company policy regarding personal records and how the policy is to be administered and enforced.

A Day in Court

Records are a principal form of evidence used in judicial and administrative proceedings and in internal, external, or government agency audits. They provide a trail of evidence that may be more trustworthy than the memory of witnesses regarding increasingly complicated business transactions. Lawsuits concerning events of one, ten, or twenty years ago must rely more on records than witnesses. And when a legal proceeding involves the word of one against the word of another, a favorable decision is more likely for the party who can make the better showing in court through witnesses and documents.

Companies with high turnover and those experiencing fast-paced and extensive change will need to rely more on documents than witnesses. The originator of a record may no longer be employed or may not otherwise be available as a witness.

A New York Court of Appeals found a written document of a verbal agreement to be more trustworthy than the memory of a telephone conversation. When one party disputed the terms of a deal that was made over the phone, the court said that written confirmation of the conversation is the only reliable evidence of transactions where the likelihood of remembering the details of any one agreement, among scores of similar deals each day, would be small.

A witness normally sets the foundation for admission of a document into evidence. This could be the person who created or received the document, the individual responsible for a department, or even the records and information manager.

CONSEQUENCES OF IMPROPER RECORD-KEEPING

A well-functioning records and information management program ensures the existence of valuable and legally required records that will support claims by the company and defend against others' claims. It also reduces costs and exposure to liabilities by destruction of records that are no longer necessary or valuable. Without appropriate record-keeping practices, a business may discover that it has too many records, not enough records, or records that are not admissible as evidence.

Too Many Records

Business executives and corporate attorneys tend to want to keep every record "in case we're sued." However, this defense strategy could backfire on a company.

In addition to the unnecessary records storage and handling expense, the document production process for any litigation will be all the more costly and burdensome.

The Quick 'n' Dirty Company was faced with thousands of liability claims and class action lawsuits. The corporation had a record retention schedule, but it had failed to implement it prior to initiation of the legal actions. Warehouses full of paper and microfilm records had to be searched in an effort to locate records relevant to the actions. The records found on microfilm had to be produced in paper format for the opposing parties and for the court proceedings. The cost simply to produce these paper copies was $250,000.

Retention of records for periods beyond business and legal requirements also may senselessly expose a business to additional liabilities when those documents are taken out of context in a legal proceeding, or if they contain unfavorable or damaging information. Because records of a creating party are considered an admission of truth by that party, they carry more weight in a courtroom and are being used more and more to the advantage of opposing parties. Older documents are easily taken out of context, and contemporary documents are subject to misinterpretation.

The author is not advocating destruction of potentially damaging or unfavorable records. Destruction of records must be performed according to a formal record retention and destruction program that is based on an established record retention schedule and destruction procedures performed in the normal course of business.

Not Enough Records

Attorneys cannot adequately represent a company when records are not properly created and protected. When documents are destroyed before their time, or when some and not others are retained beyond stated requirements, a business may suffer negative consequences in both civil and government actions.

If a business has no proof of action or of compliance with the law, it may not receive favorable treatment from an administrative agency or civil court. Or a business may be forced to settle or pay claims when documents critical to its defense or its claim cannot be found.

The Quick 'n' Dirty Company delivered more than $5,000 worth of equipment to another firm, but was having difficulty obtaining payment. Because Quick 'n' Dirty could not produce the sale agreement or even proof of delivery of the equipment, it decided to write off the equipment as a loss, given that it would be fruitless to file an unsubstantiated claim in court against the company.

Failure to comply with a court or government agency order to produce records may result in one or more of the following consequences:

- obstruction of justice charges
- contempt of court charges
- a court's inference that documents were destroyed in bad faith because they contained damaging information
- a finding in favor of the party obtaining the order

The following scenario, based on actual case law, shows how the absence of a systematic records destruction program cost one corporation $10 million.

Except for the destruction of potentially damaging records, there was no evidence presented to the court by the defendant that employees complied with any document retention procedures. Useless and unacceptable documents were retained, but important documents could not be produced because they had been disposed of at an earlier time. Finding no evidence of document destruction pursuant to a consistent and reasonable policy, the judge concluded that the company intentionally destroyed documents to prevent their production, thus preventing a fair hearing of this product liability case. The defendant was prohibited from introducing evidence in support of its defense, and the judge issued a default judgment in favor of plaintiffs, for $10 million.

Trustworthiness Challenges

Business has a responsibility to create and maintain records that meet the conditions of trustworthiness and admissibility, as defined in federal and state laws and rules of evidence. Records considered more trustworthy are:

- records of fact—not opinion—prepared by an experienced person
- created at or near the time of an event by a knowledgeable person
- created in the normal course of business
- created and maintained to serve an independent business purpose
- created and maintained to meet a legal requirement
- created by an independent third party
- created before litigation is foreseeable

Testimony by the creator of the record, the records manager, or other qualified witnesses may be necessary to show that these requirements are met. A company also may be called upon to establish in court the existence of a records management program.

When charges of fraud are highly probable, as in financial transactions, an original record will have a higher degree of reliability. When a more accurate determination of age and a handwriting analysis are necessary, the original paper record is preferred by the technical experts performing the analysis. And a paper document bearing the author's signature will have far more evidentiary weight than the text produced from a word processor—especially when the document's author is unavailable as a witness.

A number of record forms are admissible as evidence, though some media may be more susceptible to challenge than others. (See Chapter 11, "Integrating Media Choices," for more detail on various record forms.) When the trustworthiness of a record is challenged, the party producing that record as evidence will have the burden of proof of authenticity and trustworthiness. If a record is a duplicate, its owner must be able to show that it is an accurate reproduction of the original.

The House of Good Intentions intended to produce a number of documents from its paper, microfilm, and computer records as evidence for a court proceeding. The opposing party decided to challenge the authenticity of those records. In response, The House of Good Intentions produced documents about how its records program was developed and how it operates. Among this documentation were written procedures for microfilming, audit trails of how computer records are created and processed, and certificates of authenticity for its microfilm and electronic image records.

The easier it is to alter or remove data from a record without detection except by a technical expert, the less likely the record will stand up to a challenge to its accuracy and trustworthiness. As a result, there may be difficulties regarding dependence on computer records as evidence. Until there is clarification in the courts, issues of trustworthiness may be addressed by appropriate record creation, processing, and production procedures, as well as documentation of those procedures.

The trustworthiness of records may be determined by the procedures used to create, maintain, and produce them. The methods necessary to authenticate records will vary slightly from one information system to another. In general, a records program that typically produces trustworthy records can document the following activities as having occurred in the normal course of business:

- written records policy and procedures
- development and administration of records retention schedule
- audit trails of procedures to create, process, and produce information
- certifications of authenticity for document reproduction processes, such as filming and electronic imaging
- records management training activities
- records program audits confirming that what was supposed to happen did in fact happen, and any remedial action taken as necessary
- sanctions for employee noncompliance with records policy

LITIGATION STRATEGIES

More and more attorneys are advising their clients to implement a records management program. These same attorneys are challenging the records management program of their adversaries.

The records called upon during pretrial discovery and as evidence during a trial may be a blessing or a curse. If the records contain sufficient data substantiating the company's claims, charges against the business may be dropped or a reasonable settlement may be reached. Or, they may contain information that may be used successfully by the opposing party. How well records are created, maintained, and destroyed will determine how well the program reduces certain risks and losses from any court proceeding. Based on an assessment of costs, risks, and benefits of various record-keeping practices, legal counsel can determine the best approach that provides flexibility within the legal, ethical, and practical constraints.

Records program elements that may be addressed by litigation strategies include:

- media selection and administration
- information security and preservation
- indexing and organization for efficient retrieval
- records retention and destruction

Media selection and administration may be affected by government requirements regarding record forms and rules of evidence. Information security, preservation, and indexing requirements also may be found in laws, regulations, or contracts. Records must remain in existence for as long as they are required by law or are necessary to demonstrate compliance with the law.

The next scenario is based on one of the earliest court cases that demonstrated how an IRS audit is a foreseeable action and how the absence of appropriate measures to safeguard information may be considered irresponsible destruction of records.

The records of a liquidated firm were left in the care of one of its partners, who stored them in the basement of an office building. Two years after the firm's liquidation, a basement flood caused substantial damage to the basement's contents. The firm's books and records were discarded along with damaged merchandise and other stored items. The judge determined that this seemingly careless treatment of records at a time when they were needed by the IRS supported the inference that the information would have been harmful to the defendants.

Retention Decisions

As discussed in Chapter 10, "Records Retention and Disposition," various laws and regulations specify a retention period for certain records. In the absence of a clearly stated records retention requirement, a business will want to analyze other legal considerations in order to develop strategies that impact records retention.

Essentially, risk analysis and a best effort to interpret the law will lead to appropriate decisions on what records to create and how long it is reasonable to maintain them in order to protect the business and to show compliance with the law. Legal counsel must consider the costs and risks, along with the benefits, of storage of various records groups versus the destruction of those records.

Government requirements to maintain records of company policies and procedures state only that they must be maintained long enough to demonstrate a pattern of activity and regular compliance with the stated procedures and policies. The ForwardThink Corporation accumulates several binders of policies, procedures, and program documentation for its records management program each year. It would prefer not to have to keep all of the records accumulated since it began doing business 15 years ago.

Because ForwardThink's business is a regulated industry, the likelihood of government audit or investigation is greater than for other businesses. ForwardThink also regularly is a party in lawsuits involving large dollar amounts, and it may be vulnerable to challenges of its records management program by opposing parties. The corporate attorney recommends that retention of records management program documentation for ten years is a reasonable time for preservation of the ability to demonstrate that regular procedures have been followed consistently and as normal business practices.

Records destruction programs hinge on the premise that nearly any corporate document—no matter how innocent it may seem—may become a weapon in the hands of an opposing counsel. A carefully developed and administered document destruction program is especially important to a business likely to be involved in litigation. It can be most effective in defending against antitrust charges, employee claims, or product liability disputes, because these cases often are won or lost on the strength of incriminating documents uncovered by a grand jury or a plaintiff's counsel in discovery. A proper document destruction program might eliminate any incriminating evidence.

However, a degree of risk is involved in a decision to destroy records prior to any legal requirements or prior to the expiration of an applicable statute of limitations. A statute of limitations establishes a time period during which a claim may be filed, so a litigation strategy to retain records for all or part of the time period will be based on the importance placed on protecting the company's right to a proper defense against any claim and to file a claim against another party.

Legal counsel must weigh the costs, risks, and benefits to determine the most reasonable retention period for individual record groups. But even the lawyers do not always agree on legal strategies regarding retention. The strategy to retain records as long as possible is based on the assumption that the records will be more helpful than harmful to the company. Others argue that if the records do not exist—and their nonexistence does not violate a law or create an adverse inference—no charge may be brought against the company.

Somewhere between these two extremes is probably the more reasonable approach. There certainly will be circumstances in which retention of specific records for the entire statute of limitations is advised. If a company is likely to be a plaintiff, or if an adverse party would have sufficient information to file a claim without the need for discovery, it may be best to retain relevant records for the full statute of limitations. If the risk of a claim and loss against the company is small or nonexistent, or if there is little prospect of being a plaintiff, counsel may advise retention of records only long enough to meet business needs because the high costs of storing the records outweighs the risks of any losses.

A federal requirement states that job application records for permanent positions must be retained for one year to satisfy age discrimination record-keeping requirements. The House of Good Intentions has decided to retain these records for a longer time period in order to be able to defend itself against claims under other employment discrimination laws that have longer statutes of limitations periods.

Legal counsel may determine that the retention of records for the full statute of limitations time period would create an unreasonable and an extraordinary burden.

ForwardThink Corporation has a large volume of project files that contain project administration records, which are not subject to any statute of limitations, and project support documentation records, which are subject to a statute of limitations of six years. The agreements with contractors may prove useful in the event of litigation by showing the liability on the part of those contractors for any defects in manufacturing, construction, or design.

The administrative paperwork is maintained separately from the contract documentation so that the administrative records may be assigned a shorter retention period than for the contract records, facilitating the destruction process. ForwardThink's business need for the administrative records is only one year after the close of the contract and its business need for contracts is only three years.

A review of the past ten years indicates that any lawsuits or other legal issues related to the contracts normally were initiated within four years after the conclusion of a contract. Weighing the risks and benefits of the nonexistence of the records after a different number of years, ForwardThink's legal counsel determines that given the low probability of a claim after four years, and the savings involved in records storage costs, the company could withstand a loss of up to $50,000 and still break even if the records were destroyed after four years.

The risks of a shorter retention period also may be appropriate when the statute of limitations is in a state in which the company does little business or when the statute of limitations is deemed excessively long compared to those of other applicable states.

Though there is no federal requirement to retain production records more than three years after its product is produced, The House of Good Intentions distributes large quantities of the product to several states that have statutes of limitations for personal injury. All but one of these statutes of limitations begins after distribution of the product. That state has a statute of limitations that begins at the time an injury occurs.

Because its product has a useful life of up to ten years, the company's liability for injury could be for as long as sixteen years after distribution of the product. If the company decides to retain its records for the longest period of time, it would be retaining its production records longer than necessary for the other states. This would add to records storage costs and extend exposure to claims in other states. A risk analysis determines that most injury claims of a significant dollar value occur within the first five years after distribution. The final decision by legal counsel *is* to retain production records for seven years.

Rules of Evidence

Managers should become familiar with the federal and state rules of civil and criminal procedure that apply to their particular business:

- the Uniform Business Records as Evidence Act, adopted in 16 states, allows a record of an act, condition, or event to be submitted as evidence if its custodian or another qualified witness testifies to its identity and mode of preparation, and if the record was made in the regular course of business at or near the time of the activity.

- the Best Evidence Rule allows the submission of a duplicate record as evidence only if the absence of the original is satisfactorily explained.

- expanding the Best Evidence Rule, the Uniform Rules of Evidence and the Uniform Photographic Copies of Business and Public Records as Evidence Act (UPA) give duplicate records and microforms the same legal status as an original record under certain conditions in federal proceedings and in those states adopting both laws.

A computer printout shown to accurately reflect the data is considered an original record. Government agency regulations may vary regarding any record forms and their technical requirements for records that are subject to investigation and audit. Computer output microfilm (COM) is treated as a computer record, or original, by some agencies, while others treat COM as a microfilm, or duplicate record. A duplicate record may be admitted into evidence in place of an original provided the duplicate accurately reproduces the original and the authenticity of either is not questioned.

The IRS has rules for both microfilm and data processing records. Microfilming must meet industry standards, procedures must be documented, and the film must be preserved. The capability to produce a visible, legible record must exist for as long as the record remains material in the administration of any IRS law. Summary computer reports are allowed, but the detail must be readily available. All support records must be identified and made readily available.

A 1986 modification of computer record regulations included a new requirement to maintain computer records in a retrievable, machine-readable form for review by the IRS. System documentation and an audit trail of the steps from data entry through printout are necessary. Media must be clearly labeled and maintained in a secure environment with backups maintained off site. Periodic inspections of storage conditions and the condition of tapes will ensure information integrity. The IRS must be notified immediately of damaged or lost computer information.

Not yet specifically stated in various rules of evidence are the conditions under which video, electronic mail, voice messaging, electronic document imaging, and other relatively new record forms are admissible as evidence. A business must anticipate what the legal requirements may be based on existing rules of evidence. However, the use of imaging has been tested successfully in various courts.

Business use of video in the courts most often is in personal injury cases, but the potential of video to support or challenge a business could become greater in other areas. The same technology that exposes crimes of bank robbers, police, and congressmen also could be used to frame innocent companies through selective taping or high-tech tampering. The growing millions of video camera owners, being spurred on by the "video vigilantes" portrayed in the media, are unhampered by today's court requirements that only law-enforcement officers may obtain warrants and that the consent of one party must be obtained prior to planting hidden cameras.

Discovery

It has been estimated that 80 percent of the time and expense of a typical lawsuit involves pretrial examination of facts through discovery. The intent of the discovery process is to help the parties prepare to litigate by cutting down on the number of surprises, and frequently it helps them decide to settle before going to trial. Often, however, discovery is the source of needless delay and expense, and it is sometimes used as a weapon against an opponent. The costs to a business when an opponent demands too much are:

- higher attorney fees
- the potential invasion of privacy
- the risk that the opponent will stumble onto something useful—in the proper or improper context

There are litigators who seek as much material as possible in pretrial discovery, and they do not have to prove their case to do it. Unless the victim protests, an adverse party may use this strategy as an economic weapon or may misuse the information.

During the document production process, one company president was dismayed by a request for financial and customer information, along with other trade secrets and proprietary information. The firm's president feared the misuse of the information as a competitive advantage, and he suspected that his adversary was using this tactic as a form of harassment. Unaware that he could protest the request for proprietary information, he decided to settle the case out of court—even though the company was innocent of the charges made against it.

In a typical lawsuit, there may be a formidable volume of documents in the possession of the business, adversarial parties, and third parties. These records, in varying conditions of quality and states of organization, may be scattered throughout a number of locations.

Warehouses or rooms of paper have been filled by cases involving complex financial transactions, liability, technical product development, engineering or construction projects, long-term pollution allegations, and multiple plaintiffs and defendants. The following are examples of the paperwork burden experienced by different companies:

- Hiring a large crew to search for and copy documents may cost as much as $20,000 each week.
- The direct cost to one employer to retrieve, copy, and deliver documents required by an EEOC subpoena was an estimated $75,000.
- The securities firm, Drexel Burnham Lambert, Inc., spent well over $40 million to copy, collate, and cross-reference 1.5 million pages of documents for its insider trading defense.

- One attorney rented a U-Haul truck to carry his client's files across the country to the trial site.

- Perhaps overdoing it a bit, 150 attorneys shipped 680 cartons of documents to the FTC overnight on a rented DC-9, in response to antitrust regulator requests for information on a $25 billion acquisition of RJR Nabisco, Inc.

All relevant records must be collected, organized, and maintained so that they are readily accessible throughout the course of a proceeding. Among these litigation records are:

- pleadings (the plaintiff's complaint and the defendant's answer or counterclaim)
- company records for review in case preparation
- written objections to the court for a protective order or to limit discovery
- documents produced by both parties in discovery and records to track document production
- sworn depositions of witnesses
- interrogatories and answers
- physical examinations
- trial briefs, transcripts, and other records

A litigation case management firm describes the document review and production process in a typical case:

More than one million documents, averaging two to three pages in length, are available for review in the search for records relevant to the proceedings. These records may be located in a number of facilities and locations across the country. Case attorneys determine the document selection criteria used to identify just under 200,000 documents subject to a more detailed review by legal counsel. Counsel selects records that may be needed to make a case, to respond to requests by the opposing party, and to create a case management database. Critical records are then retrieved, copied, and delivered to the appropriate parties. An estimated 50,000 deposition documents and 4,000 listed trial documents are added to this database. Of all of these documents, only about 30 are considered key trial documents.

More often than not, an opposing party will attempt to include a broad statement of records covered in the hope of getting additional useful information. A business may request clarification when a subpoena is too broad in scope, and a court may then narrow the scope or clarify the types of information covered in order to reduce unnecessary hardships and to prevent one party from uncontrolled rummaging around in the records of another party.

The House of Good Intentions just received notification that the IRS will audit a tax return filed four years ago. Assuming that the IRS will routinely request an extension to complete the audit, legal counsel for the firm is requesting clarification of what area(s) will be audited. Upon receipt of this clarification, the remaining volumes of tax records for that year that are not subject to the audit may be released for destruction according to the firm's retention schedule.

LITIGATION SUPPORT

It is estimated that for an average case a records manager will spend up to four weeks, full time, coordinating records litigation support activities with attorneys. A good records program helps reduce excessive disruption of normal business activities by:

- routine records destruction according to a retention schedule
- organization of the remaining records for their timely retrieval and production at the lowest costs
- prevention of unnecessary losses caused by the inability to find key documents

A records management computer system can be especially useful for timely and accurate records retrieval.

Prior to installation of a computer indexing system for the records of a casino-hotel, retrieval of records for a grand jury investigation of a hotel guest normally took three people and three days of searching through boxes. After system installation, copies of room and telephone charges and other guest records can be located in a matter of minutes. The records staff and auditors were especially appreciative of the new system when the casino-hotel was hit with three simultaneous audits: internal, IRS, and one from an outside accounting firm.

A more advanced records program has a step-by-step guide for the discovery process, from locating records for review and document production through the litigation proceedings and beyond. A few programs have a special procedure for premature record destruction, discussed in Chapter 10, "Records Retention and Disposition."

Document Hold

A legal, investigative, or tax hold on records is a procedure to suspend destruction of records related to foreseeable or pending litigation or government investigation. Even if no legal requirements exist to create or maintain a record, that record cannot be destroyed within established, routine records destruction procedures.

Irresponsible destruction of records related to a legal action greatly increases the risk of being forced to settle a claim or of other losses in the proceedings. Any indication at all of an existing action or one looming in the future is a signal to cease document destruction, or the violating party may be subject to charges of obstruction of justice. An adverse inference may arise if a party proceeds with records destruction when it knows—or should have known—the documents are relevant to an action. It also is illegal to knowingly permit record destruction by others or to advise their destruction.

To reduce the risks of loss or alteration—unintentional or otherwise—many businesses remove the relevant original records to a secured location, leaving duplicate copies in their place for normal business use. Additional security procedures may be implemented as appropriate.

A 1991 lawsuit that blames asbestos insulation products for a variety of respiratory illnesses suffered a serious setback before jury selection was even completed. The suit involved 9,000 plaintiffs and 10 different defendants, and more than 50 prospective jurors had been screened after three weeks of painstaking selection by both parties. A defense team psychologist had prepared a document that analyzed the prospective jurors, and a defense attorney's employee inadvertently faxed this revealing document to a plaintiff's law firm by mistakenly pressing a speed dial number. That law firm in turn faxed the papers to other plaintiffs' lawyers.

Though the defense argued that the document was a privileged work product, the judge found that the defense had not taken reasonable precautions to prevent the mistake, thus constituting a waiver of confidentiality based on attorney-client privilege. But because this particular disclosure threatened to taint the entire trial, the judge dismissed the prospective jurors, and ordered the jury selection process to begin again.

Document Production

Failure to produce records required by a subpoena may result in court charges and penalties such as:

- obstruction of justice or contempt of court
- sanctions imposed by the court
- adverse inferences that may be harmful to the violating party

When the court believes that a company has intentionally withheld evidence, the court could rule in favor of the opposing party, as in the following case.

The largest ever judgment of bad faith against a major insurance company occurred early in 1991. The insurance company had not complied with the plaintiff's requests for documents and records. The judge found that the discovery abuses were knowingly and willfully carried out with a view of preventing the plaintiffs from obtaining relevant evidence, and held the insurance company liable for the entire face amount of the policy. Jurors, with a history of favoring the individual over large corporations, were left to determine the punitive damages against the company.

A subpoena duces tecum, the order to appear and produce documents, may be for a proceeding to which the recipient may or may not be a party. It is best to refer any subpoena to legal counsel for the appropriate response as soon as it is served or received. Corporate attorneys and outside counsel may turn to one of a handful of litigation support firms across the country for case management services. To avoid expensive and disruptive changes as the case proceeds, it is best to decide up front which activities will be handled by in-house legal staff, outside counsel, or a litigation support services firm.

Unless a subpoena specifically states that records are for use outside the office, it is preferable to furnish the records for on-site examination. Copies should be prepared that show only such detail as is specifically requested. Documentation regarding the summons and what information was furnished should be maintained in the event this information is needed later.

An effort must be made to produce documents in a timely and organized fashion for an opposing party in litigation.

Lawyers for 300 plaintiffs accused the defendant of employing a strategy to slow the exchange of information. The attorneys complained that some of the defendants' 8 million pages of documents in a warehouse have nothing to do with the targeted product in this liability case, and that the manufacturer is withholding relevant records. The judge concluded that the defendant "created a haystack and now invites the plaintiffs to find the needle," and ordered the defendant to produce the documents in an organized fashion.

The capability to retrieve documents is critical to a company's own case management. If a document is not found because of poor filing, the company may wind up unprepared when the opposing party produces the record, or it may lose its case. Experts in litigation case management note that accurate, detailed indexing and efficient organization of records may provide savings of thousands of dollars, along with the ability to prepare detailed complaints and responses months earlier than otherwise would have been possible.

The coding, indexing, and cross-referencing system used to track documents may be manual or automated, and may vary according to the nature of the case. Objective document coding and indexing extracts only information that requires no judgment, such as names and dates. Subjective document coding and indexing requires a ranking of the document for its relative merit, coding the issue(s) addressed in the document, and creating an abstract. Automated systems that may be used are database or text management, optical character recognition, or imaging systems.

ForwardThink Corporation used a document imaging system to help control more than 115,000 documents, or one-half million pages of text, for one of its cases. In a matter of minutes, the system helped attorneys locate a single page of a document that forced the opposing party to offer a $35 million settlement.

Protective Orders

From traffic court to the Supreme Court, court records normally are open to the public. So are most congressional hearings. Transcripts, testimony, evidence, and judgments of criminal and civil cases are available. Records that routinely are not available to the public are those of cases involving juveniles, adoption, some unresolved criminal cases, trade secrets, and records protected under the right to privacy. Certain state courts allow disclosure of records only when the requestor has a demonstrated legal interest in the case, when the requestor is a taxpayer in the state, or when there exists a potential business relationship with one or both parties.

A business will need to show good cause before court records are sealed. Requests to seal court documents are routinely approved as long as both parties agree. A judge reserves the right to consider the public interest in the determination of whether to seal court proceedings and documents. Records generally not sealed are those considered to be of public interest, including those dealing with possible health, environmental, and other public hazards. A movement is afoot in a number of states to make it more difficult to seal court records and settlements, especially in product liability and other civil damage suits.

5

The Bottom Line

A competitive advantage being sought by many businesses is manage-ability at the lowest costs for responsiveness, quality, and service. An enterprise must be able to anticipate, recognize, and quickly respond to changing business conditions and adversities. A company's records and information systems contain valuable data and knowledge for intelligent business decisions, risk management, and compliance. In today's com-petitive, regulated, and litigious environment, a business should take the same care managing its information resources as it does managing its employees and assets.

A business can only get by without good record-keeping practices if it:

- never needs to find a record after it is filed
- never is sued or investigated
- never has to file a claim for lost or damaged property

Good records management practices identify and safeguard valuable, useful, and legally required records in all media that are necessary to manage and protect a successful business. They also prevent the unnecessary accumulation of records and the premature destruction of records. The fewer and better records that are retained are organized and stored in ways to ensure prompt availability when needed, at the lowest costs possible.

Along with the benefits associated with record-keeping are burdens and expenses in terms of human resources, equipment, and facilities.

The higher the quality of records management, the lower the costs to create, collect, store, protect, and produce information.

To earn the highest return on the investment, proper management should begin when records are most valuable and most at risk—in their early phase of life. A comprehensive records and information management program provides a higher return on the investment by contributing to a company's profitability through:

• reduced risks and expenses
• timely response to changing business conditions
• streamlined internal processes and higher productivity
• enhanced services, products, and effectiveness

This comprehensive program is described in more detail in Chapter 12, "Organization and Staffing for the Records Function."

RISK MANAGEMENT AND RECORDS

A company's records and information, and how well they are managed, will impact certain business and legal risks, including:

• loss of revenues, assets, or business
• loss of legal rights
• exposure to losses and penalties in litigation or investigation
• violations of the law

Because the costs of poor record-keeping generally remain hidden, few companies have established a comprehensive records management program to limit the associated risks. Eventually, the losses do show up on the bottom line. Worst-case scenarios when records issues are ignored may be:

• costly inefficiencies
• unnecessary exposure to liabilities
• monetary and other losses

Records management is a function of risk management when it is designed to minimize the risks related to information security threats and government or court actions. It provides for a proactive approach to potential adversities, rather than a knee-jerk reaction in a crisis. Risk analysis weighs the costs, benefits, and risks of various record-keeping practices against the relative value of various records groups. Such an analysis identifies those practices that will provide the most flexibility within the legal, ethical, and practical constraints.

There may be risks associated with the existence or the nonexistence of certain records. A business will want to ensure that certain records continue to exist in order to protect the organization and its assets and to minimize any risk of losses. This does not always translate to keeping everything for all of eternity. Because many records lose their value over time, a business has the right to dispose of records no longer required by the government or law in order to meet its own needs of efficiency and reduced costs and risks.

The relative value of a record depends on its true purpose(s), which may be to:

- support business decisions and activities
- analyze and manage business risks
- preserve rights and protect assets
- represent business assets

The need for conscientious record-keeping practices is greater in a company with a higher dependence on its information systems and intellectual properties, and in a business with a higher probability of government investigation or litigation. Legal counsel should establish criteria for what record-keeping requirements may be reasonably followed and what practices would create an exceptional burden.

- What records truly merit protection because of their content and value?
- What are the risks if the information is available, if it is not available, or if it falls into the wrong hands?
- What is the likelihood of litigation or investigation, and for how long?
- Will there be sufficient evidence for a defense or to file a claim?

More detailed information on information security, assets protection, and litigation strategies is found in Chapters 4, 7, 8, and 9.

WHITE-COLLAR PRODUCTIVITY

In this fast-paced and volatile marketplace, efforts are turning to the improvement of white-collar productivity. Efficiencies and better productivity translate into lower costs. Simplification of internal processes allows for more systematic attention to other business fundamentals, such as making decisions and responding to customer needs.

New technologies already have proven to be capable of reducing certain labor costs, and there is potential for even higher returns on those investments. Instead of more workforce reductions, the next wave of cuts will be in the work load, through the use of technologies to help business work smarter. Management will be able to use the time and effort formerly devoted to the location or production of information for the analysis of the information.

New technologies provide the capability to redesign internal processes and structures. As critical, up-to-date, and accurate information becomes more readily available to more end users, organizations are flattening their structures to gain the flexibility to adapt quickly to new opportunities and challenges. Internal processes are being streamlined by the elimination of procedures, reviews, and other time- and energy-consuming activities that may interfere with primary business focuses.

The productivity of knowledge workers is not necessarily measured in terms of volume of work produced, but it does directly relate to the ease with which information sources are accessed. In offices where the workers have free access to information and each other, productivity takes on a more qualitative nature. There is more efficiency and effectiveness, or more of doing the right thing right.

Information makes employees' jobs easier. Duplication of efforts is reduced when there is prompt access to current information. The quality of products and customer service may be improved when current and accurate information is readily available to workers. Misinformation or the lack of information causes errors, or it may result in no action when action is necessary.

Management, professionals, and other office workers should be spending more of their time in their areas of expertise instead of looking for information.

If 25 percent of a professional's time is spent tracking down the right information, and that professional's annual salary is $50,000, the annual cost to the company for ineffective use of that professional's time is $12,500. In a company with 200 professionals, the hunt for information by professionals costs is $2.5 million each year.

See the next chapter for more on how records and information practices promote efficiencies during the corporate change process.

Information Retrieval for Better Productivity

Information is only as good as the ability to put it to work in a timely manner. Timely access to decision support systems may reduce the time it takes to bring a new product or service to market, to enter a new market, or to build market share. If a business does not know it has certain information, or the information cannot be found, it is of no use to the company.

Improved access and selectivity may be required so that senior management may access the right information at the right time for a fast and appropriate response to changing business conditions. When value-less records are maintained, the human resources necessary to file, sort, retrieve, and maintain those records are wasted. When records are not organized for efficient retrieval, records users have to sort through useless information to get to the good information.

Better information retrieval rates will contribute to higher productivity. Application of records and information management principles at the beginning of a record's life will save time and dollars later, limit liabilities, and ensure consistency over a longer period of time. There are a number of ways to initiate long-term efficiencies at the time that a record is created:

- select the most appropriate record form
- keep files current and accessible to those authorized for access
- organize and index records so they may be found again once they are stored
- include in or on documents any file codes, form numbers, or other useful information to help facilitate proper filing
- include a statement directly on a document or printed form about the proprietary or private nature of the information
- determine where the official copy will be maintained to eliminate the creation and maintenance of unnecessary duplicate copies

A critical aspect of information management is not where one puts the information, but whether the information may be found again. Easy-to-use retrieval systems are required. Individual employees and departments tend to develop their own indexing and filing systems in the absence of a standard system. But what happens when the employee resigns or when another department needs the information? Will a record be found again once it has been placed in a file cabinet or on film or on a computer disk?

Thinking ahead to the time of information retrieval will determine the appropriate media and the proper design of indexing and filing systems. Indexing and filing systems that are understood and used by employees will improve retrieval and storage efficiencies; common terminologies and cross-references will quickly locate desired information and identify unnecessary redundancies.

The House of Good Intentions has an extensive collection of 20,000 slides, 10,000 negatives, 2,500 photographs, and 6,000 video tapes. Until the collection was indexed and cross-referenced, searches for a specific photo or slide were consuming far too much time. Frequently, out of frustration and time constraints, the same photography shots were retaken. After indexing the collection, the firm reported a cost avoidance of $10,000 each month.

The design of filing systems for speedy and accurate information retrieval begins with an indexing system. Certain equipment configurations then provide more efficient office design and access to records. (Equipment is discussed in more detail later in this chapter.) Inactive records are removed from prime office spaces to records centers so that users do not waste time fumbling through or around inactive records to find the needed active records.

How records are arranged within filing systems will affect retrieval efficiencies. Filing rules and name authority guidelines will be needed when an alphabetical arrangement is used for low volumes of records. Without consistency in the forms of names and in alphabetic arrangement, records users may easily overlook important records in the system. Numeric arrangements reduce the chances of filing error and work best when the numbers used are less than five digits. Alphanumeric arrangements are the most typical arrangement method used to more efficiently accommodate larger volumes of records and minimize problems with sequential filing.

The use of color coding on records containers also improves efficiencies and accuracy in a manner similar to the uses of color coding on electronic components, electrical wiring, and theater tickets. Manufacturers and users of color-coded labels report from 30 to 50 percent faster and simpler filing and retrieval. A visual scan of color-coded rows of files, computer tapes, or microfilm cartridges for a break in a color block will easily find a misplaced record. The consistencies and bright colors in an open-shelf environment also present a more professional and attractive appearance in the office.

If a company with 100,000 files has 5 percent misfiles, essentially there are 5,000 lost files. What if one of those 5,000 files is a sales contract worth thousands or millions of dollars?

Media selection also affects access and retrieval rates. Paper is the most labor-intensive record form to retrieve and store, and misfiles are more likely with paper records than with microfilm or computer records. The fixed continuity of the files on microfilm reels, cassettes, or microfiche prevents a certain amount of misfiling or the loss of individual records. Computer data and imaging systems also eliminate misfiles and can locate information faster. By reducing filing or data errors, work steps may be eliminated.

Installation of an electronic imaging system in one business cut the number of work steps from twelve down to three, reduced the number of errors, increased productivity by more than 50 percent, and improved response times to customer requests.

A major airline installed an electronic imaging system for information that is used by its mechanics. By reducing the time it took for mechanics to find the necessary information by 75 percent, the airline saw planes returned to service faster and it realized an annual labor savings in excess of $1 million.

Standards for Better Productivity

Most businesses tend to use a single system and uniform procedures for its personnel, accounting, and computer functions. Standards help reduce errors and duplication of effort. The same rationale of using standard practices to promote efficiencies and quality also applies for records and information management.

Typical areas for development of records and information management standards are:

- indexing, organization, and filing systems
- technical terms
- procedures
- media selection
- equipment and supplies specifications
- storage facilities
- vital records protection
- records retention and destruction
- information security
- computer applications

The following scenario describes what can happen in a company without indexing standards and coordination of records in different forms.

The TechTrack firm's search for all records related to a specific government contract for an upcoming audit is hampered by the lack of a corporate-wide index to records in all media. Further complicating matters is the fact that each record form's indexing system is based on different terminology, so records creators and records users are not talking the same language or using common search strategies. Staff must seek management information systems (MIS) department assistance to check for any relevant mainframe computer records. Then they must go to each department to search paper files and check the numerous individual indexes to desktop computer data files. The microfilm collection must be searched box by box, and a records search request must be transmitted to TechTrack's records storage vendor in hopes of discovering any inactive records related to the government project.

A business also is better capable of implementing change in its records and information systems when standards are in place throughout the enterprise. Training of personnel is easier, and the process of opening, closing, or consolidating office sites is simplified.

The House of Good Intentions has 25 offices across the country, all of which have compatible indexing and filing systems. These indexing systems are based on a single subject listing of records, instead of on the organizational structure. When the firm acquired another company to expand its marketing capabilities, the new subject areas were simply added to the records indexing system.

As business conditions in different markets changed, some offices were closed or the business operations were consolidated with others. Because the records in all facilities were organized and filed in the same manner, they were easily consolidated with other records in their new location. In certain states, the business was to be sold to other companies, and the gathering of customer records, contracts, and financial information for analysis and determination of a fair sale price was quick and efficient.

Technological Applications

Records and information management computer systems are automated indexing and tracking systems that manage and control records for improved efficiencies and accuracy. Records are processed faster and with fewer errors as their movement is easily tracked between users, locations, and record forms. The computer generation of labels and overdue notices reduces administrative tasks. Systems also support management activities with data and information about the records and the program. When a system is media-transparent, it is possible to identify all relevant records in all media in all locations.

More advanced systems will forward records requests to a records center, or will retrieve the electronic or microfilm image from the same work station. Many systems produce instructions for records transfers, vital records, media conversions, valuable or sensitive records, litigation, and records destruction. Other systems index the results of legal research for record-keeping requirements, expediting legal counsel review and approval of a records retention schedule. Such systems also help uncover overlapping requirements and make it easier to update the research in the future.

Bar coding is a particularly useful method of processing and tracking records. The paybacks from the use of bar coding are increased speed and accuracy.

To Your Health, like other insurance companies, is paper-intensive. More than 200 files are requested daily by sales, accounting, and marketing personnel. Until recently, the files were scattered throughout the facility, and up to 15 percent of the files were misfiled or were not checked out properly. The staff dedicated to finding these missing files were spending four hours each day trying to track them down, and the delays in getting back to the customer were sometimes three to four days.

To Your Health decided to install a bar-coding system to track its files. Ten temporaries applied bar code labels to file folders over one weekend. Now, when a file is removed, a pen scanner reads the file folder's bar-code label and either the employee's identification card's bar code or the bar code for the destination that is posted on a wall chart. This data is downloaded to a personal computer three times a day. The list of missing files was significantly reduced when the new tracking system provided a find rate of 98 percent, and the files search staff was reduced by two full-time positions. The investment of $30,000 for the personal computer, software, initial tape run and other incidentals was paid back in one year by hard dollar savings. The soft dollar savings was a bonus.

REDUCE OR AVOID COSTS

Records management practices may result in both one-time and ongoing savings and cost avoidance. Improved productivity, as discussed earlier in this chapter, may result in cost avoidance and cost reductions. The greatest impact on measurable cost reductions or cost avoidance comes from a reduction in the volume of records and from the cost-effective management of facilities and equipment. In addition, good record-keeping may reduce the professional fees charged by accountants, attorneys, and other outside professionals. Appropriate protection of records will prevent excessive costs to reconstruct lost records or prevent other liabilities when records are prematurely destroyed.

Reduce Volume of Records

The volume of records may be reduced by:

- avoidance of the creation of unnecessary records and photocopies
- elimination of unnecessary records
- conversion of paper records to microform
- conversion of paper or microform records to a computer form

When a business has fewer and better records, the unnecessary exposure to liabilities is eliminated, and efficiencies for storage and handling of the remaining valuable records are improved. Valuable office space is then available for the more current records, for people, or for other important business activities.

At home, a packrat mentality is a nuisance. In business, it is costly. Companies with file cabinet flab have high costs for records storage, equipment, facilities, retrieval, handling, transportation, and lost data. They also suffer more expense and a higher risk of other losses related to document production for litigation.

In a typical organization that has not implemented policies and practices to control the growth and volume of its records, anywhere from 20 to 50 percent of its stored records are duplicate, obsolete, or unnecessary records. These valueless records should be destroyed because of the expense to store them and because they may become financial and legal liabilities in other ways.

Computers, photocopiers, and telefacsimile machines have made a significant contribution to white-collar productivity. But these office technologies also contribute to an explosion of paper, the most expensive information carrier to maintain. The convenience and relatively small expense to produce duplicates has resulted in mountains of unnecessary paper records.

Once a record is filed, filmed, or entered onto a computer, it does not self-destruct under normal storage conditions. A planned, deliberate program to physically remove and destroy records on a regular basis will control records growth. Without that, a business will continue to squander its limited resources on records that are no longer useful, valuable, or required. Chapter 10, "Records Retention and Disposition," discusses the development of a records retention and destruction schedule.

The House of Good Intentions decided to purge its office of file cabinet flab and unnecessary trash. The records slated for elimination were identified by the newly developed records retention schedule. Out went 45 tons of records and 350 barrels of miscellaneous items, including abandoned shoes, vases, and coffee mugs. Many of the remaining files were microfilmed, and 370 boxes of records were sent to storage. Within the first year, not one request came in for the records that had been destroyed, confirming the excellent job done on development of the records retention schedule. Files are now current, and filing and retrieval times have been reduced.

Copy Management

The proliferation of unnecessary duplicate records continues to be a significant barrier to the successful management of records and information. The wide array of high-quality copiers and printers is both an asset and a detriment to effective communications within an organization.

Better copy management will reduce the time and expense of photocopying and computer printing, as well as the storage expense of useless or redundant records. A central filing system also helps reduce excessive duplication from individual departments duplicating and storing other departments' records. If a company is able to prevent a record from being created in the first place, it will avoid the expense of its reproduction, filing, distribution, and the time spent reading or handling the record.

The Quick 'n' Dirty Company discovered that a large number of unnecessary duplicate copies had accumulated in files that were about to be microfilmed. Based on a random sample, it calculated that $450,000 in salaries and benefits and $600,000 in equipment and supplies had been spent on the production of these now unnecessary copies. Storage and handling costs over the years for these duplicate paper records were not measured. Because there was no time or staff to search and remove the duplicate records, the firm went ahead with the filming of the records, creating additional unnecessary expense to the film processing and its storage.

Forms and Reports Management

Forms and reports management are management functions that control the design, production, and distribution of forms and reports. Thousands of dollars, hundreds of hours, and hundreds of square feet of space may be saved by the proper management of reports and forms. Both forms and reports have high costs in terms of creation, distribution, storage, and use. Questions to be asked about every form and report are:

- Is it necessary, or could it be consolidated with another form or report?
- Could it be redesigned to improve its efficiency?
- What are the costs to create, copy, and distribute the report or form, and is it worth it?
- Could the frequency or number of copies of a report be reduced?
- Could a report be distributed on microfiche or by electronic mail?

Media Choices to Reduce Volume

The selection of a record's medium impacts space and equipment requirements and shipping costs. A jukebox, or computer library of optical disks, consumes approximately the same floor space as a photocopy machine, but it holds enough document images to fill 200 four-drawer file cabinets. The costs to ship microform are less than those for paper, and the transfer of computer data is the cost of a long-distance call.

For the best return on the investment, records are created in the form that satisfies all business and legal requirements, or they are converted to another medium as early as possible in the record's life.

The TechTrack firm replaced almost 9 million pages of paper documents with microfilm. The cost avoidance figure of $280,000 is based on the difference between the production and storage costs for the paper system and for the microform system. Another 120,000 documents were scanned to an electronic imaging system, reducing space and equipment costs by $200,000. At the same time, it implemented a computer output microfilm (COM) application that resulted in an annual cost avoidance of $2 million for space, personnel, and hardware.

See Chapter 11, "Integrating Media Choices," for more information on specific record forms.

Cost-Effective Facilities and Equipment Management

Office space in corporate America is a major expense in terms of construction, rent, furniture, equipment, utilities, maintenance, insurance, trash hauling, and other costs. The more efficiently the space is used, the more cost-effective it will be. The facilities commitments for records and information may be reduced by:

- reduction of the overall volume of records
- transfer of records to lower-cost facilities
- conversion of records to media that require less space
- use of high-density equipment to store records

Permanent and inactive records may be removed to less costly facilities when they are no longer necessary for daily activities. Industry studies indicate that typically as much as 33 percent of a company's records are appropriate for storage. To identify inactive records, usage can be tracked by a computerized records management program, or a records retention schedule may serve as a guideline for when designated records groups may be converted to another record form or when they are no longer active. (See Chapter 10, "Records Retention and Disposition.")

Off-site records centers are one of several less expensive storage alternatives. A records center stores records in uniform-sized containers on shelves much higher than those allowed in an office space, providing a capability to store five times as many records per square foot. If a business cannot justify the cost to use its own facilities for its inactive or vital records, a commercial records center may be appropriate. Commercial facilities typically have the security and environmental controls necessary to protect vital records, computer tapes, and other record forms that are sensitive to adverse environmental conditions.

The records center in the headquarters office of The House of Good Intentions is running out of space as its accounting files grow in volume and age. The cost to duplicate its existing high-density shelving system on site would be $30,000, but there is a possibility that the headquarters office may relocate within the next two or three years. The monthly rent for the firm's warehouse space across town would be $500 for the records storage. Monthly labor costs for filing and retrieval from this warehouse would be $500, and there would be a one-time expense of $600 for stacking boxes. Instead of these alternatives, the firm elected to send its records to a local commercial records center, where the initial cost of boxes would be $400 and the monthly storage and services charges would be approximately $200.

For the remaining active records in prime office space, a business may increase the volume of records stored by judicious selection of media, filing supplies, and equipment. For example, elimination of hanging files to separate and store file folders may increase the amount of available filing space by 20 to 50 percent, depending on how the hanging files had been used.

Vertical file cabinets are adequate for small departments and offices, but they become inefficient when the volume of records exceeds four file cabinets. Lateral file cabinets consume more wall space than vertical file cabinets, but they do not require as much valuable open floor space per filing inch. Most lateral cabinets available today may be adapted for storage of various media other than paper files, and they may be converted for installation as a high-density, mobile storage system.

The ForwardThink Corporation is relocating a department to another facility. The department has 5,000 file folders and hanging files in roll-out drawer, vertical file cabinets. The 17 cabinets consume 116 square feet of floor space, which would be an annual cost of $2,900 in the new facility. As new equipment and furnishings are being purchased for the new facility, the company considers the elimination of the hanging files and the use of lateral file cabinets in the new facility. Because hanging files are an expensive supply that served no real purpose other than to consume filing space, the decision is made to eliminate them. Lateral filing cabinets are chosen for the new space because of the reduced space requirements and lower cost per cabinet and filing inch. They also will work well in the new open-plan office area. The 5,000 file folders, without the hanging files, will require 10 lateral file cabinets and 34 square feet in the new office space, at an annual space cost of $850. The file cabinets in the existing facility will be transferred to other departments where they may be needed, or they will be sold as surplus equipment.

Open-shelf records storage units use more vertical space than file cabinets, as they are six or eight shelves high. They also are more efficient because more than one user at a time may access their contents and there is no time lost to the opening and closing of drawers. Like lateral cabinets, open-shelf storage units may be modified to accommodate a mixture of record forms by the installation of shelves, bins, tubs, hanging bars, tape racks, drawers, or other accessories.

If a company has a large volume of records to be stored in a small space, high-density shelving is the best alternative. In these mobile storage systems, shelving sections or storage units are supported by carriages on tracks for movement of the rows to create aisles where they are needed. These systems may have manual, mechanical, or electrical operation controls. They provide the capability to use 50 to 70 percent less floor space for the same volume of records. High-density systems are not recommended for very active records because of the inability to access all records at once.

Figure 5.1 illustrates the differences in space requirements for the same amount of files when they are stored in filing cabinets, in fixed open shelves, or in mobile shelving units. Both the fixed and mobile

Figure 5.1
Filing Systems Space Requirements

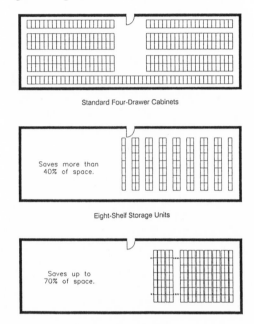

Standard Four-Drawer Cabinets

Eight-Shelf Storage Units

High-Density Mobile Shelving

shelving systems shown actually have an additional 820 inches of filing space than that available in the filing cabinets shown.

Motorized files or carousels also are available for records storage. These systems bring the files to the user. They are much more expensive in terms of cost, installation and maintenance, and access is limited to a single operator. Costly facility modifications may be required to support the additional weight of high-density storage systems.

Various configurations are possible for high-density systems to fit existing space and to accommodate different forms of records. A leasing arrangement may make a system affordable to certain businesses. The higher the cost per square foot of the space, the quicker the return on investment for a new system. High-density systems may be even more cost-effective when the only other alternative is new construction.

Standards for Volume Purchase Savings

Significant dollar savings may be achieved by establishment of standards for supplies and equipment. Standards provide the opportunity to set up agreements with vendors for volume discounts.

In its first year, TechTrack opened 25 new offices across the country. Corporate standards were established for its equipment, supplies, vehicles, facilities, signs, and other assets. Among the records-related equipment and supplies were file cabinets, a filing supplies starter kit, paper shredders, and a personal computer and printer for the records management computer system. The ability to purchase these supplies and equipment in volume resulted in a savings of $70,000 that first year.

More and more businesses are prohibiting the use of legal-size paper in order to realize savings in:

- filing supplies and equipment
- storage space requirements
- photocopier supplies and capabilities
- convenience in storage and handling

Over-sized documents can be reduced to standard paper by a photocopy machine, and large computer printouts can be replaced by letter-size paper or microform with the necessary computer configurations.

GENERATION AND PROTECTION OF REVENUES

Records and information management is a cost center, but there are a few areas where it may be directly tied to revenues. The protection of certain intellectual properties and vital records safeguards future income, as discussed in Chapter 2, "Preservation of Legal Rights and Business Assets." The types of records to be safeguarded, and information security practices, are described in more detail in Chapters 7, 8, and 9.

The disposal of waste may be transformed from an expense to an income-producer. Companies that come up with imaginative solutions to trash disposal may have a jump on their competition, as businesses eventually will not have a choice about its trash. They may even find that recycling does more than clean up the environment and their corporate image. It may pay off in dollars and cents. When a business recycles its trash, it not only earns dollars, but it reduces its trash hauling and landfill fees. A 1990 survey by the International Facility Management Association found that more than half of the reported recycling programs claim a recovery of up to $50,000 per year, and 3 percent of the programs are recovering $100,000 or more every year.

A company may help alleviate the public crisis of rising landfill costs, along with the trash in them, by recycling and by demanding recycled products. Laser printer cartridges may be recycled through reconditioning, thus reducing cartridge costs and waste. Records systems may use file folders, hanging file folders, and boxes that are manufactured with recycled paper. Because tinted paper is not easily recycled, a business may choose to switch from the traditional yellow paper pads and other colored papers to white paper and recycled paper.

The demand for paper is rising—even in this age of computer technologies—and most of that paper eventually ends up in a landfill. A corporate center with 500 people may generate at least one ton of paper each week. Paper shredders are increasingly being used for more than document security destruction. They are used to turn refuse into packing material, avoiding the expenses of bulky styrofoam "peanuts" and trash hauling. Or shredded paper is compressed into bales as recycle-ready material.

6

The Roles of Records in Corporate Change

The tidal wave of mergers, acquisitions, and takeovers of the eighties has subsided and changed somewhat in nature. Merger activity is focusing more on cross-border deals than domestic acquisitions, and is motivated more by long-term, strategic considerations than short-term, financial considerations. Strategic alliances are picking up where today's mergers and acquisitions leave off. Other changes affecting business today are a continuing effort to be lean and mean through downsizing or restructurings in order to adopt the capabilities of new technologies or respond to changing market conditions. Facility moves also are under way as companies continue to search for better business or real estate conditions.

Managing change is complex and challenging, and a business needs responsive, supportive information systems. Business must be able to respond quickly to changing conditions and expectations among a wide range of constituents: customers, employees, government, stockholders, suppliers, and the general public. Good information systems help identify those changing conditions, and they support the necessary business response. The potential of records management support services for designing and implementing business change should be exploited—not ignored. How well a records and information management program is designed will determine how well it supports the business throughout the change process from the point of conceptualization and decision-making through operations under the new business conditions.

Records and information systems help ensure compliance with relevant laws and regulations, and the fulfillment of obligations to individuals and other entities. This becomes especially important during times of change, which tend to breed more litigation and government investigation. A business may need timely access to records created prior to the change, records that document the change process, and records after the change in order to defend itself against charges or to file any necessary claims.

NEW BUSINESS VENTURES: ANALYSIS TO CLOSURE

The demand for information retrieval, processing, and production increases during each phase of business change:

- analysis
- negotiations
- decision-making
- implementation
- post-change conditions

Records and information management activities should be closely coordinated with the activities of legal, finance, and other departments, along with the activities of any outside advisory resources. Whether buying or selling, accurate and complete records of assets and liabilities must be assembled for review and analysis by the teams of attorneys, accountants, and others.

Information Security

Whenever joint ventures, strategic alliances, mergers, or acquisitions are considered, there will be the sharing of sensitive and valuable records and information between the parties involved. This information is disclosed to the potential buyers, who may be competitors, customers, employees, suppliers, or investors. Outside professional advisory services also may need access to extensive financial and proprietary information to assist buyers in their analysis of the proposal. These parties may be accounting firms, investment bankers, business brokers, acquisitions specialists, or business appraisers.

This opportunity to learn about technologies, management, and financial status may become a serious risk to a business—especially if a deal goes sour. An enterprise will want to protect itself and its secrets in order to prevent the takeover of a joint venture, unfair advantages to another party, or unauthorized disclosure of the information to others. Encoding of certain information may reduce the risk somewhat, but every individual or organization that will be in possession of sensitive or valuable records should sign a confidentiality agreement that provides for the protection of the company's privacy and intellectual property.

Publicly held companies also will want to take special care in guarding information about the proposed venture. Improper disclosure of information to outside parties, or improper use of that information, may result in charges of insider trading.

Business Valuation

Activities preparatory to a sale begin with an accurate valuation of the business. To determine a fair asking price for the business, or the portion(s) of the business to be sold, records will be required to identify assets, liabilities, and any other obligations, such as warranties or other agreements. Even the archives of a business may be treated as an asset in the negotiation of a sale, or as a tax write-off if a decision is made to donate the archives to a nonprofit organization.

A potential buyer will want to evaluate the past track record, present outlook, and future potential of the target business. Other records that may be needed include:

- marketing plans
- management practices
- policies and procedures
- organization charts
- personnel files
- information on the financial and legal circumstances of the current owners

Records will be assembled, processed, and created for the critical financial and legal audits necessary in this evaluation process. Also appropriate may be an analysis of external information regarding current and future market conditions that may impact the business.

In a financial audit, a wide range of financial records from the preceding several years may be compiled for review, and new records may be created for the review in the following areas:

- profit and loss statements
- debts
- mortgages and leases
- utilities and other expenses
- status of various tax filings and payments
- bank accounts and safety deposit boxes
- securities and cash equivalents
- age, cost, depreciation, and insured value of assets
- age of accounts receivables
- monthly sales for 36 months
- sales fluctuations over 12 months
- accounts that may be lost with a change of ownership
- intangibles that may generate profit (patents, franchises, etc.)
- age and turnover of inventories
- production and labor costs
- price lists, discounts, previous increases
- employee benefit plans, insurance and wages payments
- insurance coverage types and premiums

A legal audit also will require the review of a number of company records. Documents of title and public records may need to be scrutinized to confirm that the assets for sale are free of encumbrances and restrictions on their use. Are there any pending or foreseeable claims, lawsuits, or government investigations? Are there any contingent liabilities, such as warranted products? What is the extent of compliance with various government requirements for safety, labor, environment, wages, taxes, retirement plans, and more? What are the rights and obligations stipulated in contracts, agreements, leases, permits, and licenses?

Among the documents and information required for other legal considerations are:

- a list of all states where the target company is qualified or authorized to do business
- deeds and titles
- intellectual properties, including trademarks, patents, and copyrights
- product or service agreements and warranties

- powers of attorney
- contracts for the purchase of materials, supplies, and equipment
- lists of creditors

The following illustrates how inaccurate and incomplete records expose a company to the risk of lawsuits from its customers, subcontractors, and acquiring company.

A national telecommunications firm decided to sell its business operations and customer base in a number of states so that it could concentrate on a targeted region of the country. When the time came to assemble an information package for potential buyers, corporate headquarters found it had to resort to estimates of business value. The inventory records of fixed assets, vehicles, equipment, and materials were current and accurate, but not so were the records of the rights and obligations of the company, its subcontractors, and its customers. A corporate database reflected one picture of business commitments to customers and subcontractors, while the original agreements and warranties to back up that information were incomplete and inconsistent.

As the analysis and negotiation process continues, additional records are processed and created on top of the existing records made available for review. Financial models may be developed to evaluate a number of different scenarios. The effects of alternative structures or the timing of a transaction on taxation may be documented for study. There may be other records created in support of certain legal considerations, and records may be produced for disclosure to certain parties or filed with a government agency in order to comply with a government requirement.

Government Requirements and Legal Considerations

Throughout the analysis of a proposed acquisition or merger, government requirements or other legal considerations will compel the review, creation, or disclosure of certain records. The burden of compliance with antitrust, securities, taxation, environmental, consumer protection, and other legislation must be assessed. Issues of timing, financing, and other strategies must be considered.

There may be a requirement of prior notification to the Department of Justice or the FTC regarding a merger or acquisition. The shareholdings of a target business may need to be traced to ensure compliance with SEC regulations or appropriate blue sky securities laws of the state(s) involved. A merger may require approval by the seller's shareholders and the shareholders of the buyer, unless the buying corporation already owns a majority of the stock. There are a number of federal and state laws that require a franchisor to disclose designated information to a potential buyer within certain time frames associated with the payment of deposits and the signing of an agreement.

Mergers of companies that are competitors or that produce similar goods or services will need to pay more careful attention to antitrust regulations than mergers of companies that will form a conglomerate. An advance review of business plans for proposed operations or mergers by the Department of Justice will ascertain whether they involve risks of criminal prosecution. Document filings with the Department of Justice's antitrust division or the FTC will be required when a merger or acquisition meets certain legal criteria, including transaction size and the degree of control being acquired.

There may be other legal or government actions necessary before final closure of a deal. Businesses may need to be prepared to justify their actions in response to government investigations or complaints from competitors, suppliers, customers, or shareholders. There may be actions taken by others against one or more parties that result in a temporary restraining order or preliminary injunction, litigation, or further government investigation. The existing records and new documents that may be required for any litigation or investigation will need to be organized, indexed, duplicated, and forwarded to the appropriate government agencies or a court.

Contracts and Agreements

When one business takes over another business, it typically takes over its assets, customer base, data processing systems, product and environmental liabilities, tax exposures, and other hidden liabilities. A business sale contract typically specifies:

- assets to be sold
- assignment of responsibility for various liabilities
- purchase price
- financing arrangements
- any noncompetition or consulting arrangements

• provisions for arbitration

A sale agreement may or may not stipulate that certain or all debts and liabilities will be assumed by the buyer or will be retained by the surviving organization. However, clarification of which assets and liabilities are and are not part of the agreement is critical to the avoidance of lawsuits further down the road. Separate employment contracts often are used in supplement to a sale agreement to ensure the retention of key personnel.

It is highly recommended that a clause be included in a sale contract that specifically addresses the responsibilities of each party for the business records in all forms—paper, microfilm, electronic, and so on. In the absence of a clause that speaks to records responsibilities, the assumption is that records responsibilities will go to the party that assumes the relevant assets, liabilities, or obligations as designated in the terms and conditions of the sale contract. Any large volume of inactive records should be mentioned in the agreement, as it may represent a significant expense to the party who will be responsible for the maintenance of those records for as long as they may be needed for legal or government purposes.

Under the agreement, the target company may be responsible for preparation of records for the new owner by organizing, consolidating, segregating, and even duplicating and packing the affected records. Time frames should be established for any duplication and transmittal of the records to support the acquired portions of the company. Procedures and responsibility should be determined for any necessary records and information searches resulting from the fact that designated records were not provided at the time of cut-over.

AFTER A MERGER OR ACQUISITION

The newly formed organization will need immediate access to important company data from all acquired segments in order to support its assumed customer base, assets, legal liabilities, and other terms and conditions of the agreement. Timely integration of the various information systems into efficient, well-functioning systems is critical to the reconciliation of differences between the old and new organizations while simultaneously maintaining stability and effectiveness.

Information from each company is required to identify and resolve transition issues, including:

• identification and notification of all customers and suppliers

- elimination or consolidation of redundant or obsolete business functions and activities
- determination of personnel requirements for the new organization and qualifications of existing personnel
- management and resolution of different employee pay scales, benefits programs, and retirement plans
- disposition of duplicate assets, including equipment, vehicles, and properties
- collection and indexing of documents relevant to pending and potential litigation and government investigation regarding the merger, as well as activities of the individual acquired companies
- development of budgets and realistic timetables for transition activities

Information demands will continue at a high level under postacquisition conditions. At the same time, there normally are problems with information retrieval because of incompatible or inadequate records and information systems. The preacquisition planning process and sale agreement may or may not specify what records will be made available to the new organization. Incompatible methods of collecting and organizing data may present difficulties for the timely access to useful information. A business may need to seek outside assistance from a computer and software business that specializes in helping merged companies consolidate or separate their electronic information.

Disposition of Records

The parent company, former board of directors, general partners, or owners normally are personally responsible for the maintenance of a company's records when an organization is totally dissolved. The records to be maintained are those that may be required by government regulations or court proceedings, and they must be maintained for the time period necessary to meet those obligations. These individuals may be sued or fined for any violations of legal record-keeping requirements.

When the disposition of the acquired company's records is not clarified by an agreement, that responsibility normally is determined by default. Records related to specific legal responsibilities, debts, and obligations should be retained by the organization that assumes those burdens. Certain records may be required by more than one organization if assets and obligations are divided among the organizations. The new owner should identify records associated with the assets, liabilities, and other business functions it now has assumed, based on the sale agreement, to determine the proper disposition of records.

When The House of Good Intentions acquired the subsidiary of another business, property and equipment leases were renegotiated or officially transferred through the individual vendors and lessors. Lists of the acquired products, parts, and equipment were forwarded to the House of Good Intentions, along with ownership documents, tax records, and user manuals related to those assets.

Though The House of Good Intentions did not assume either the customer liabilities or revenues related to transactions prior to the sale, the firm requested duplicate copies of selected customer files to support its efforts to continue providing products and services to those acquired customers. Because some files contained records that were the property of the customer, customer agreements regarding records were updated to reflect the records transfer to a new business. Because The House of Good Intentions did not agree to assume responsibility for any past employee actions related to the employees that it agreed to hire from the former company, only basic employee records were duplicated and forwarded to The House of Good Intentions: name, address, length of service, job title, and salary.

If an audit of the target company's records during the acquisition analysis was not practical or feasible, the new owner should initiate a records audit immediately after the close of the sale. If the former organization had a records management program, the records document-ing the program will need to be retained in the event of litigation or investigation regarding records from that company. It is preferable to do a records inventory before the records are shipped to the new organiza-tion, so that the active records may be organized and packed separately from inactive records. Removal and appropriate destruction of duplicate and other valueless documents will avoid unnecessary transportation expense and reduce storage and handling costs.

If the acquired records are well indexed, it may be possible to compare those records with the new owner's records inventory to identify any duplicate or similar files that may be easily consolidated—especially customer or vendor files. All other active records must be clearly and accurately indexed and labeled so they may be merged with those of the new owner and maintained in the same manner as those records.

The Quick 'n' Dirty Company came into being as the result of a merger of three separate businesses. Three trucks dumped business records into a warehouse several weeks after the merger was finalized, and there were no packing lists with the boxes. Many boxes containing folders, binders, and diskettes had no labels. The company was falling behind in payment of its bills because the supporting records were nowhere to be found and because the firm's cash flow was reaching critical conditions. A team of temporary employees had to be hired, trained, and sent to the warehouse to find the records necessary to collect on past sales transactions and the records necessary to generate new sales from the existing customer base.

The inactive records from an acquired business normally are maintained separately from the active records. A system to retrieve these inactive records must be established so that they may be easily recalled for the inevitable audits, government investigation, or litigation. If the former organization had no records retention schedule, one must be prepared for the eventual destruction of records after they have met tax, government, and legal requirements.

DYNAMIC COMPANIES AND THEIR RECORDS

The more dynamic—or quickly changing—a company, the more difficulties it will have keeping its information systems current and responsive to its end users, government requirements, and legal obligations. Government investigations and litigation tend to increase during organizational change, and records must be readily available for these proceedings. Records and information security also becomes more urgent when an enterprise is expanding, contracting, or relocating. When a business changes, grows, or shrinks, easy-to-use records and information systems become even more critical as energies of a changing workforce are diverted to new endeavors.

Growth and Change

A start-up business often experiences a fast pace of change and growth in its first few years. Ideally, a records and information management program should be established along with other internal systems and processes at the time of start-up.

The House of Good Intentions began business operations with five employees and grew to 1,200 within two years, in 25 office sites. As early as one month after incorporation, the firm hired a consultant to design a corporate-wide records and information management program. The consultant worked with top executives and managers to establish a subject listing of anticipated or probable records groups for purposes of indexing and coding its records. An outside law firm used this list to research record-keeping requirements and develop a records retention schedule. A records manager was hired later to continue program development and to coordinate records activities in each facility through the office managers, designated as the records coordinators.

A corporate information security policy was established for implementation in every facility. Responsibility for certain records management tasks was assigned to corporate headquarters, relieving field offices of these responsibilities. A standardized filing system was designed, which later proved to simplify the opening, consolidation, and closing of facilities as the business matured. Records transfers between locations required no additional processing other than changing the location data field on the records management database.

As a business changes, the records and information management program must be updated so that it may continue to support changing business functions. A well-designed records and information program will be dynamic enough to adapt easily to organizational change so that it may continue to be compatible with and supportive of new organizational directions.

One retailer experienced spectacular growth, from 2,000 square feet to 40,000 square feet within only a few years. Along with the physical expansion of its inventory and facilities was an explosion of its paper-based information management systems used to track its inventory of 200,000 items, 9,000 vendors, and thousands of customers. A customized computer information system was installed to maintain a current inventory and to enhance services to its customers.

Facility Moves

Facilities relocations present many challenges and opportunities for records and information management. The challenge is not to disrupt daily activities any more than necessary. A relocation also is an opportunity to settle into a new location with a new or updated records and information management program in place.

Good planning for an office move begins far in advance of the move and should involve the records manager. The records manager determines how much space, types of equipment, and any special environmental requirements will be necessary for the various records forms. Unnecessary and valueless records should be purged to eliminate the expense of moving them to the new facility. To further reduce space requirements for records in the new facility, it may be appropriate to transfer inactive records to a records center or to convert designated records to microfilm prior to or during the move. If a move is across state lines, the records retention schedule may need to be revised to reflect the record-keeping requirements of that state.

Security measures will need to be stepped up in preparation for a move, during the move, and throughout the settling-in period. If employees resign or are terminated as a result of the move, the probability of employee sabotage is greater. Security threats also increase from outsiders during the chaos and confusion of a move.

Workforce Reductions, Facility Closures, Sales of Business

When a business decides to tighten its belt or change its market focus, it often turns to workforce reductions, facility closures or consolidations, or the sale of part of its business. Similar to the determination of whether or not to buy another company, records are required to analyze what tasks, jobs, functions, or business sites may be eliminated within the new business strategy. Because of the higher risks of litigation or government investigation—especially regarding employee actions or agreements with other parties—more careful attention will need to be given to accurate and complete record-keeping throughout this change process. Government information disclosure requirements also may be applicable, as in the federal law that requires 60 days' notice to employees and local governments of any plant closing or major layoff, or an employee's right to continue health insurance coverage.

Surviving employees of a workforce reduction do not need excessive burdens as they take on expanded responsibilities with fewer resources. Decision-makers may find it easier to cut a larger number of lower-paid positions than a smaller number of higher-paid positions, but they may be short-sighted when they cut too deeply into staff and clerical positions and the higher-paid managers end up spending too much time on routine chores, such as correspondence and reports production. The principle that elimination of work and streamlined internal processes should go hand in hand with the elimination of workers also applies to a records and information management program, which should always be easy to learn and use, within the legal and practical constraints.

When a facility is closed for reasons other than a sale of the business, the company remains responsible for the assets and liabilities of that facility's operations. The tendency on the part of many enterprises is to dispose of records from a facility as part of its closure procedures. However, without the records necessary to clarify its position, it would be difficult for the business to defend itself or to file claims against another party should the occasion arise.

The House of Good Intentions decided to close one of its facilities as a result of its poor business performance. Prior to the closure, final paperwork was processed on invoices and customer billings, and suppliers were notified of final billing procedures. Records of employee terminations or transfers to another site were created. Technical manuals, handbooks, and other company information and property were collected from those employees to be terminated. Additional records were created during the closure process to document the disposition of records, vehicles, furniture, equipment, hardware, software, and other assets.

The data on personal computers targeted for sale as surplus equipment was transferred to tape, and the hard drives were reformatted to completely erase the data. Duplicate and other unnecessary records were destroyed. Certificates of records destruction, records transmittal notices, and all other records created during the closing process were collected for retention, along with other records from the facility. They were transferred to a temporary staging area set up at corporate headquarters for the records most likely to be recalled within 18 months for financial, legal, or customer relations uses. All other records were transferred to a records center until they may be destroyed per the records retention schedule.

7

Sensitive and Valuable Records and Information

Gordon Gekko, portrayed by actor Michael Douglas in the popular film *Wall Street*, declared that the most valuable commodity is information. Though he was referring specifically to insider information, records and information may be valuable to a business in a number of other ways. Some of those records, under certain circumstances, also may become a liability in some way.

A business owns sensitive and valuable records and information that are in need of protection from damage, loss, and unauthorized disclosure. Safeguarding such records can preserve rights under the law, fulfill legal and other obligations, and prevent losses. In the normal course of business, a company might be in possession of another party's records and information, which must be treated in much the same way as the company's own records. When certain business records are not properly protected, any loss or damage could result in legal actions, the inability to rightfully collect money due, loss of competitive advantages, or other consequences.

This chapter defines the types of records and information that are valuable or sensitive, and it presents a variety of possible threats to information security. Chapter 8, "Records and Information Security," provides specific guidelines for the protection of records and information.

WHAT TO PROTECT

At the heart of business records are those with real or potential financial, administrative, operational, or legal impact on the business. Business records also may have historical importance. Or a business may be in possession of records and information that are the property of others.

Some records have more value than others, and the sensitivity of certain records may cause harm when they are disclosed to the wrong parties. Every business has valuable and sensitive records and information. Valuable records are those that affect income and profit or that represent a tangible asset. Sensitive records are those which must not be disclosed indiscriminately to others, within or outside of the organization. A method to classify business records helps identify the various levels of sensitivity and value. Clearly stated guidelines for each classification then prescribe how those records should be protected. A record can be both sensitive and valuable, and its classification within these two categories may change as circumstances change, or after a designated time period.

Unfortunately, the terminology used to describe sensitive and valuable records and information has not been standardized within the business community. "Confidential" may be used by some businesses to describe sensitive records that are dubbed "private" by others, and "private" sometimes is used to include "proprietary" information. "Proprietary" and "trade secret" are frequently used interchangeably, though, in the true meaning of the word, proprietary is a broad category that includes trade secrets. Until standards exist, the needs and preferences of an individual organization—along with consideration of privacy, security, and secrecy issues—best determine how the categories of value and sensitivity are defined. For purposes of discussion in this book, classifications of sensitive and valuable records are described in the next sections.

Private Records and Information

Private records and information are those that are sensitive and should not be disclosed indiscriminately within or outside the organization. Disclosure usually requires the prior approval of the record's owner. Employee and customer records are typical records in this classification, and a number of federal, state, and local record-keeping requirements exist regarding such records. They specify the types of records to be maintained, for how long, and guidelines for the proper use of and access to these records. Privacy issues are a primary concern regarding employee records, which contain personal data. Customer records may be subject not only to privacy regulations, but also to proprietary restrictions and other government regulations.

Litigation and Investigation Records

Records and information relevant to any potential, current, or past litigation or government investigation are considered sensitive and, in some cases, valuable. To summarize from Chapter 4, "A Day in Court," such records must be retained for the duration of the action, and normally for a specified number of years after the case or investigation has concluded. These records must be protected from alteration or loss, and a number of restrictions may be necessary regarding their disclosure.

Vital Records

In the event of a natural or manmade disaster, certain business records are critical to the organization's ability to continue operations or to resume business after the disruption. These records, and any records required to handle the crisis situation, are considered vital records in that they preserve the company's rights and help fulfill company obligations. Chapter 9, "Records Vital to a Business," describes in more detail the business records and information required to resume operations and to ensure continuation of the business entity.

Historical Records

Business records, as the corporate memory, provide an accurate portrayal of business development and activities over time. Examples of records that may be considered historical include:

- advertising materials
- architectural drawings
- board minute books
- financial records
- materials unique to the business or industry
- newsletters and other publications
- officers'/executives' correspondence

- oral histories
- photos
- scrapbooks and clipping files

Each business determines the relative value of corporate history and the extent to which historical records are to be collected, indexed for future reference, and preserved. Historical records are frequently used as original source materials for biographies or histories, or for public relations and marketing functions, such as:

- trade and other public exhibits
- museum exhibits
- corporate identity programs
- commemorative histories
- centennial celebrations

A corporate archive may be a tangible asset in the negotiation of the sale of a business, or it may be a tax write-off when donated to a nonprofit museum or university. Legal departments sometimes need historical records to document legal positions. Historical records can establish rights to a trademark registration, justify a tax position, or place legal matters in a historical context of policies and events. Knowing the chronology of product development and distribution, or the details of a product's failure or success, may become important one day.

Proprietary Information

Intellectual property is a special type of intangible personal property. It represents the scientific, artistic, creative, or commercial endeavors of an individual or an organization. In terms of business records and information, the intellectual property of greatest concern is proprietary information. Proprietary information is the broad term used to encompass various types of information that have some value to the owner. This value could be diminished or destroyed if the information is disclosed to others or disclosed without appropriate restrictions. The basic criteria for proprietary information are:

- the information is not generally known
- the information gives an advantage to the proprietor over others

- reasonable efforts are made to protect its secrecy

Proprietary information can be information, records, software, and other work products that are developed on behalf of a company or by using the company's facilities. It is information that was difficult or costly to develop, or that has an intrinsic value. Records and information that may be considered proprietary include:

- building plans and blueprints
- business plans
- customer lists
- designs, drawings, and models
- financial and cost data
- manufacturing and production reports
- marketing plans and methods
- patents
- policies and procedures
- pricing information
- software and code
- training materials

Protection for certain types of proprietary information is provided under the law in the form of trade secret, patent, copyright, trademark, and service mark statutes. A trade secret is any formula, process, method of operation, pattern, device, or compilation of technical, financial, or business information used in the production and delivery of goods and services that provides a distinct advantage over a competitor who does not know it or use it. It is usually determined or developed at considerable expense of time, effort and/or money, and is known only to those who made that investment. A substantial element of secrecy must exist so that it would be difficult for anyone to acquire the information except by the use of improper means.

A patent is a tangible asset in that patent laws grant a seventeen-year, exclusive right to make, use, and sell a new and useful design, process, machine, manufactured item or other composition, or any new and useful improvement on it. Copyright law protects an exclusive right to print, sell, and exhibit written materials, musical compositions, art works, photos, movies, television programs, software, data systems, and other creations placed in a tangible medium of expression.

Information Belonging to Others

In the normal course of business, a company may come into the possession of records that are the property of another individual or organization. Contracting organizations and those involved in joint business ventures often require valuable or sensitive information that belongs to another party—especially government contractors. (The federal government estimates that it created more than 6 million new secrets in one year, though it is not sure of the exact number, because of all the secrecy.) A business in the role of a contractor also may create or use records, which become the property of the contracting organization.

A business is responsible for the proper use and control of others' information and for compliance with any provisions set forth in a licensing agreement, contract, law, or government regulation. Failure to maintain adequate security for these records and information—including proper disposal of the documents—may result in a law violation, litigation, and other consequences.

Unless it is in the best interests of the company, it is best to avoid unnecessary possession of others' records and information, and thus any unnecessary obligations to protect such information. On the occasions when another party wants to provide unsolicited ideas, suggestions, or inventions for consideration, it is wise to formalize this submission process by requesting a written proposal that omits details prior to acceptance of full disclosure.

INFORMATION SECURITY THREATS

Threats to the security of business records and information may originate from a number of sources, both internal and external to a company. The most common source of threats originates with people. A number of environmental threats to information security exist, ranging from earthquake and tornado to power failure and fire. Even the very medium on which information is recorded (the information carrier) and the means to process the information (the information processor) may threaten continued existence of the information. Microfilm, paper, and computer systems are vulnerable to aging, adverse environmental conditions, and abuse.

Human Threats

Through intentional or unintentional behavior, human threats to information security may include:

- computer operator error
- unauthorized computer access
- filing error
- dumpster divers
- criminal activity
- vandalism

People inside a business usually are a greater information security risk than outsiders. Current and former employees have the skills, knowledge, and opportunity to cause information damage and loss, through negligent or intentional behavior.

More information is lost through accident and negligence than through sabotage or spying. Inadvertent disclosure of valuable or sensitive information occurs when an employee is careless or is unaware of what needs protection or how it is to be protected.

What are the odds of misdialing a fax number and sending information to the wrong fax machine? Pretty good, as experience shows. One business received a confidential fax communication misdirected from a law firm that was intended for a real estate broker. The documents included a detailed justification for cancelation of the residential contract and a copy of a personal check in the amount of $20,000, complete with the party's address and bank account number.

Valuable information might be left out on desks, on meeting room walls, and in wastebaskets. The janitorial staff probably knows more company strategies and secrets than any single company employee. There are janitors making more money selling trash than emptying it when they moonlight for the competition.

Businesses may go to great lengths to prevent unauthorized access to their computers, but they sometimes neglect the unshredded printout tossed into trash dumpsters, or the confidential report left on a photocopier, that could wind up in the wrong hands.

One brokerage firm found itself in an embarrassing—and legally vulnerable—situation after its trash blew onto the property of a neighboring business. When the brokerage company refused to pick up its trash after receiving complaints, the neighbor simply mailed the discarded customer balances to the brokerage firm's clients. Many customers, outraged at the irresponsible handling of their personal financial information, transferred their investments to another firm.

People love to talk about their jobs to professional colleagues, potential employers, job candidates, suppliers, and the media. Sometimes, in their excitement, they slip and reveal more than they should. Occasionally, sensitive conversations are within earshot of strangers in restaurants, airports, and trade shows. Or "need to know" becomes "everybody knows" when a conversation leads off with, "I shouldn't be telling you this, but. . . . " Such acts of negligence are much like locking a safe and leaving the valuables on the floor next to it. Though it is possible that the valuables might not be disturbed, the likelihood of loss or damage is greatly increased.

Employees who leave a company to work for the competition or to set up their own competing business also may be an information security risk. Competitors have been known to lure away key personnel expressly for the purpose of obtaining marketing plans or customer lists. Occasionally, an employee unwittingly takes records and knowledge to the competitor when unaware of their proprietary nature. Or a worker might go to the competition to spite an employer, with or without an intention to disclose proprietary information or engage in illegal or unethical activities.

Both insiders and outsiders may pose information security risks through criminal, malicious, or mischievous actions. A disgruntled worker may exact revenge on the employer.

One computer programmer saw the writing on the wall that he was going to be fired, so he tampered with the company's computer system. Two days after he was terminated, a computer virus destroyed 200,000 data files.

An employee with drug problems may steal from the company to pay for an expensive habit. Computer theft, made easier today with computer portability and mainframe power on desktops, will result in data loss. Publicity seekers may disclose information about hazardous waste management, and computer hackers may lock up a system to prove a point. Industrial spies may sell trade secrets to the competition. Criminals steal revenues from telecommunications firms by cracking the codes to access communications networks; felons embezzle money by altering manual and computer records. More often than not, perpetrators perceive their victim as an institution, so that "no harm is done to anyone."

The threat of terrorism, typically greatest to a company's operations in foreign countries, also is an information security threat. Only recently, the United States was at war with a country that poses a very real terrorism threat to business in the continental United States. Shortly after the war's end, many companies reported that security efforts would be continued out of fear of revenge or retaliation.

Environmental Threats

Threats to the security of records and information can arise from a number of environmental conditions. The greatest—and probably most ignored—environmental threat is a natural disaster such as a rain or wind storm, hurricane, flood, tornado, or earthquake. The sentiment that "it won't happen here" tends to make a business discount the potential consequences of such an event. Even if a tornado does not make a direct hit on a business, the company still may suffer serious damage if the tornado hits its power source or communications network.

A number of facility problems also could affect information security. A fire or a flood resulting from a broken pipe or failure of a sump pump could damage computer hardware and records in all media. An air-conditioner breakdown might cause an unexpected computer shut-down, or ravenous rats might cause a short in wiring and cabling.

The electrical power that lets us do things faster and more efficiently is the same power that can damage or destroy expensive equipment, cause data loss, and even cause fire. Microcomputers are more sensitive to power surges and power sags than are a refrigerator or photocopy machine. From static discharges to power spikes and lightning strikes, equipment and data can suffer immediate damage or delayed damage when the cumulative effect of many minor power surges takes its toll. Unexpected power changes can blow a circuit, scramble data, or physically damage a disk.

Media Permanence and Durability

Another real threat to information security may be the very medium on which the information is recorded. From paper, photographs, and microfilm to optical disk and audio tape, the quality of processing and materials used affects the future life of the information. The physical characteristics of an information carrier determine its susceptibility to information damage or loss as a result of environmental conditions, use, and aging.

Permanence and durability are significant issues for records that need to be retained for an extended period of time, or even for a few weeks. Of particular concern are those records classified as vital or historical, which must be retained for ten years or longer. Deterioration of many information carriers can begin as early as three years after storage under normal conditions. Abnormal storage conditions and use will speed the deterioration process.

More detailed information on information carriers is in Chapter 11, "Integrating Media Choices."

Systems and Networks

The very ease of communicating and manipulating information is what makes computer and communications systems and their data so vulnerable to unauthorized access. Conversations on cordless phones are no longer protected by privacy laws. The very objective of computer networks to provide easy access also provides the best opportunity for unauthorized access via telephone lines.

A computer disaster—intentional or otherwise—will cost time and money in terms of down time, restoration of lost data, and repair or replacement of equipment and software. Interruptions in voice mail services may cause lost sales or customer service opportunities. Banks, retailers, and other businesses depend on their communications networks to continue performing daily business transactions. And network disruption can be life-threatening if it shuts down communications traffic switching, air traffic control, medical condition monitoring, or military defense systems.

Even if a company is able to salvage its data from a disaster, it may not be ready to resume operations in a timely manner if the disaster destroyed the hardware, software, or networking capabilities required to use the data. Obsolescence of hardware and software also may play a role in the threat to the existence of information. As systems are updated and replaced, consideration is not always given to the ability to access the older data files, which may need to be retained for possible future use.

If perhaps only in the news and entertainment media, computer hackers are moving to the forefront of white-collar crime. The fun and sport of it all begins to take on a criminal tone when systems are accessed at financial institutions, businesses, telecommunications companies, and government installations. A hacker may be a current or former employee—or even a stranger from another state or another country. Hackers have the ability to copy proprietary software and data, alter or destroy data, modify software, and disrupt or shut down operations.

Media hype on the computer virus epidemic has demonstrated the potential power of viruses for all the world to see. Though the virus threat remains small compared to other security risks, the damage if one hits could be more devastating than many other information security threats. Viruses can flourish through the common practices of exchanging floppy disks and transferring files or programs through networks. Viruses are a form of terrorism in that they may strike at any time, they are indiscriminate about their victims, and it is difficult to identify the perpetrator.

8

Records and Information
Security

Business records and information are valuable corporate assets to be guarded much like cash and property. They are tools to achieve business objectives and to prevent losses. Sensitive and valuable records and information, as defined in Chapter 7, need to be protected from damage, loss, and unauthorized disclosure in order to protect the business and its assets. Safeguarding sensitive and valuable information enables a company to:

- collect monies due
- preserve rights under the law
- prevent loss of business
- fulfill legal obligations
- resume business after a disaster

Failure to take measures to prevent information loss or unauthorized access to records could affect the well-being of a company. When valuable and sensitive records are not adequately protected from loss or from access by unauthorized parties, a business could find itself the subject of any number of newspaper headlines:

- "Obsolete checks found at dump are cashed"
- "Businesses fold in tornado's aftermath"
- "Strikers quote financials"

- "Employee seeks millions for invasion of privacy"
- "Lax security bars company from future government contracts"

LEGAL RIGHTS AND OBLIGATIONS

The security of records and information may be necessary in some situations to comply with statutes, regulations, or contract or licensing agreements. These legal remedies serve to protect the rights of the information owners by defining the obligations of those people in possession of certain records and information. Failure of an information owner to make a reasonable effort to protect the information will not only jeopardize the secrecy of the information, but may also result in a loss of rights to protection under the law. The information owner may find itself unable to prosecute violations or to collect damages from those violations.

Laws and Regulations

A number of laws and regulations exist that protect the rights of information owners, define information security requirements, and spell out obligations of those in the possession of others' intellectual properties. The SEC and other regulatory bodies, such as those governing public utilities and financial institutions, require organizations under their jurisdiction to have a disaster recovery plan, which includes protection of records from disaster. The principle of attorney-client privilege, computer security statutes, and SEC regulations relate to the unauthorized disclosure of information. Specific to intellectual properties are patent, copyright, trade secret, and other laws.

Patent rights and protection laws affect patent owners as well as those in possession of others' patent information. A patent is a tangible asset to be protected from disclosure to unauthorized parties prior to its registration. A company can effectively invalidate its own patent when it does not have adequate information security procedures in place prior to filing the patent application. Any and all patent documentation is essential for an owner to defend against a potential challenge. It is a good idea to notarize sketches and notes of concepts in the early development stage to establish when an idea was conceived.

Copyright law protects copyrighted property, including print materials and books, records, tapes, films, videos, and software. A business may use copyright to protect its own work products, and it has an obligation to observe copyright protection of others' copyrighted property. Copyright violations may exist when approval or special arrangement with the owner is not obtained to duplicate another party's materials for use in training programs, to distribute copies of software for use on a number of personal computers, or to allow copies to be taken home for personal use.

Software developers turn to protection in the form of both patent and copyright laws. A software buyer is licensed to use the software under the manufacturer's terms and conditions, which usually prohibit modification, copying, and transfer of the program. Licensing agreements may vary regarding installation of a software package on both an office and home computer or installation on both a desktop and laptop computer. The law makes no distinction between copying for sale or for free distribution, and software copyright owners now have the right to prohibit rental, lending, or leasing of their software. Unauthorized duplication of software is a federal offense under copyright law, with a possible fine of up to $50,000 and up to five years in prison.

There are a number of federal and state laws and regulations in effect to control the collection, maintenance, use, and dissemination of customer and employee information. Unauthorized disclosure of such information may result in personal injury lawsuits and violation of a law. Customer records may be protected by privacy laws, any statutes applicable to proprietary information, and any government record-keeping regulations specific to an industry, such as financial services and communications. Collective bargaining agreements and federal and state laws may determine employee record-keeping requirements.

Contracts and Agreements

Contracts and agreements with other parties serve to protect the rights of the information owner and to determine obligations of those in possession of the information. Contracts with an outside party for services or a product may contain a confidentiality clause to prevent indiscriminate disclosure of certain information. Separate nondisclosure or confidentiality agreements are frequently used for employees, contractors, and suppliers.

Records that are created or maintained for others as a result of a contractual agreement remain the property of the contracting party. This custodial responsibility includes proper handling of records to comply with existing privacy statutes, other applicable laws and regulations, and any stipulated contractual obligations.

Government contractors must comply with employment, privacy, and classified information laws and procedures. Any federal contractor is subject to a large number of requirements regarding the creation of records, record forms and their technical requirements, record retention, and information access procedures. A firm doing business with the Pentagon, the Department of Agriculture, or the FCC is most likely to encounter government classified information to be restricted to those with both a need to know and the proper government clearance.

Nondisclosure agreements bind the recipient of private, proprietary, or classified information to hold that information in confidence. These agreements usually define:

- what information is being provided—it must in fact be sensitive or valuable for enforceability of the agreement
- the intended and appropriate uses of the information
- the terms and conditions for use of information
- restrictions on further disclosure
- how to dispose of any records at the end of employment or the contract

An executed nondisclosure agreement is important as both a deterrent and as a means to enforce any violations.

A RECORDS AND INFORMATION SECURITY PROGRAM

The compromise or loss of information cannot be prevented solely by laws and agreements. Nor is it always possible to prosecute and recover damages after such an event. To protect its sensitive and valuable information and to preserve its legal rights, a business must make reasonable efforts to protect its information, including:

- confidentiality agreements
- clear identification of the information
- appropriate storage of the information
- communication of protection and access procedures
- other protective measures, such as facility modifications

A comprehensive records and information security program that relies on a number of security measures is necessary to further reduce information security risks. Every business has detailed procedures to handle cash, operate vehicles, and manage other assets to prevent losses and liabilities. It only makes sense to protect its information assets in a similar manner. But because it is difficult to budget for invisible benefits, the need for information security is sometimes ignored—until a loss occurs.

Information security is a combination of loss prevention, preparedness, and recovery measures. But today's demands and capabilities for easy access to information frequently exacerbate security efforts. Security measures should be balanced with the need for a smooth flow of information in day-to-day duties, the relative value and sensitivity of the information, and the degree of risk involved. Common sense and good judgment are keys to making a program manageable.

Since a business cannot reasonably secure all records, the truly valuable and sensitive ones must be identified and protected appropriately for as long as they remain sensitive and valuable. Clear and consistent policies and practices minimize information security risks. Management commitment is demonstrated through allocation of funds and staff to security measures, a written code of business conduct, a drug-free workplace, and policy enforcement. Information security practices must be documented in the event that a company needs to show proof of its · efforts or to file charges against violators.

Information security policy should focus on the nature of the information. Focusing solely on a computer information system or a particular office location will leave holes in security coverage. Information to be protected must be found in all of its various forms and in all of its numerous locations to determine how best to restrict access.

Adequate records and information security is a combination of measures that affect employees, facilities, property, media, information processors, records disposition, and disclosure. (Procedures for the proper release of information are covered later in this chapter.)

Personnel Security

Many companies are leaking information like a sieve—primarily through employee actions.

An MTJ Teleprograms, Inc., instructional video, entitled "I Shouldn't Be Telling You This, But. . . . ," effectively communicates the message that security begins with employees. A Columbo-type investigator is hired to find the spy responsible for leaking proprietary information. Instead of a spy, the investigator discovers that information is lost because company policies are unenforced and employees are careless.

Depending on the nature of a job, a company might consider screening of job applicants and nondisclosure agreements for new hires. Employment screening to help assess potential security risks occasionally is as extensive as federal government security clearances for classified information. The legal department should retain employee nondisclosure agreements, or at least keep a list of the agreements if they are stored elsewhere, for reference if a complaint is filed or in the event of an alleged breach of agreement.

A confidentiality agreement is the first formal step toward educating employees on information security. From the point of hire and the orientation period through termination, employees should continuously be made aware of the value of records and information as company assets. Even the best security plan is useless if it is not understood or enforced. By raising information-security consciousness, a business reduces the risks of inadvertent information disclosure. Sensitive and valuable information must be clearly marked in a consistent manner, and employees need to be trained to recognize such records. Employee responsibilities regarding the receipt, handling, and usage of the company's or others' proprietary information in the course of business-related duties should be clarified in orientation sessions, security briefings, and training sessions targeting specific user groups.

The potential for employee sabotage cannot be completely eliminated, but an organization can implement deterrents, and the means to prosecute and recover damages. A confidentiality agreement and company policy may state that compliance with information security policies and practices is a condition of employment, and that failure to comply may result in appropriate disciplinary action, up to and including dismissal. Any loss, compromise, or suspected compromise of information should be referred to a security, auditing, data processing, or other appropriate group or individual for investigation and follow-up.

Information security policies and practices should be monitored and documented regularly. Documentation helps preserve the right to prosecute the theft of information by showing that:

- the information was in fact in need of protection
- reasonable measures were taken to protect the information, including employee training activities and facility security measures

- the access was unauthorized

Employee responsibilities for information security do not always end with employment termination. In fact, post termination often is the time of greatest risk to information security from an employee. The termination process may include steps to ensure that all records and information in the employee's possession are returned and that future access is denied. An exit interview may reaffirm employee agreements and even provide a new statement for signature that confirms the return of all proprietary documents, work products, access cards, ID badges, keys, and other assets. Computer system passwords should be deleted or changed immediately. When an employee leaves to work for a competitor, some businesses have their legal counsel send a letter to the competitor as notification of the employee's obligation not to disclose any confidential information that may have been acquired during employment.

Security of Facilities, Property, and Public Places

A number of security measures can be implemented for the company's facilities and property, as well as for the use of business records and information in other locations. Business travel and the growing trend toward working at home add new dimensions to the protection of information developed or used away from a designated work site. Security efforts will vary according to the degree of risk involved and the nature and value of the records and information. Several practices and security measures are suggested here for consideration:

- Clear off desks at the end of each day and lock sensitive and valuable records in desks, cabinets, safes, or rooms.
- Change locks on file cabinets containing sensitive information so they are different from the standard locks normally provided by the manufacturer.
- Discuss sensitive issues behind closed doors and refrain from using speaker phones.
- Erase boards and remove documents, drawings, flip charts, and other materials from meeting areas.
- Avoid leaving information in reception areas, rest rooms, and other public areas.
- Lock doors to offices and meeting rooms when not in use, and protect a minimum number of keys.

- Lock telephone system closets, file rooms, and computer rooms.
- Lock exterior doors after hours—or even during business hours, if appropriate—and do not prop open locked doors.
- When keeping records at home is necessary, encourage employees to protect such information, and require that all records and work products be returned upon termination.
- Prevent theft of equipment to minimize data loss and the inability to access and process information.
- Register and escort visitors and vendors, and restrict casual visitors to designated areas. Question strangers who are not wearing a badge and request a name, address, and identification.
- Restrict the use of cameras and recorders inside the facility.
- In outside facilities, meeting rooms, and public places, avoid leaving unattended any records and information processors—including flip chart sheets, memo pads, handouts, and portable computers. Do your own photocopying, post monitors at meeting rooms to restrict access, and confirm that the public address system serves only the intended room(s).
- Alert employees to information security threats at conventions and trade shows, especially through seemingly innocent conversations and the "scratch-my-back. . . . " game.
- Caution employees against inquisitive reporters, especially when asked for "off-the-record" remarks. Reaffirm the importance of information security to sales people, distributors, and subcontractors who may be excited about a new product, reminding them that a press leak would be premature.
- Avoid discussion of sensitive information in public places, such as lobbies, elevators, restaurants, train stations, and airplanes. If discussion is necessary, consider using code names.
- Discuss any security measures necessary with an advertising agency, printer, or other vendor in possession of sensitive information.

Security of the Information Medium

Information security methods may vary according to the media used, the nature of the information, usage patterns, and the length of the record's retention. Records and information must be stored in a medium that will last for the life of the record.

Permanence and durability factors must be considered for high-use records and those records for long-term or permanent retention, such as financial and legal authority records or evidence of asset ownership. All media are subject to natural disasters, planned or inadvertent actions by people, and adverse environmental conditions and handling. Chapter 11, "Integrating Media Choices," offers a full discussion of media characteristics that affect information security.

The methods of marking sensitive and valuable records and information are based on the record's classification and the record form. It is ideal to include protective markings as an integral part of the information carrier. Paper documents should be marked in a prominent position, and the marking should be visible when the document is folded or rolled. Microforms, audio and video tapes, and software programs may include a protective information marking as part of the film, tape, or program. If unable to mark a record directly, the record should be placed in a clearly marked container. Common restrictive markings are: "NOTICE: Not for use or disclosure outside ForwardThink Corporation except under written agreement"; or "PRIVATE: This information only for ForwardThink Corporation employees with a need to know."

A cover letter or statement may be needed to advise the user that the records and materials are not to be publicly disclosed without first consulting the designated originator. Photocopy control measures may include a policy to reproduce or print records only with authorization of the owner, removal of originals and copies from copy machines, proper disposition of rejected photocopies, and use of red or a special magenta-colored paper, which cannot be photocopied. All notes, copies, and rough drafts of sensitive materials should be treated in the same manner as the final record until their proper disposal.

Care should be taken when transmitting records. Employees must not remove materials without prior approval when required, except in the regular course of business. Specially marked envelopes and other transmittal containers should be used. Private records should be hand-delivered within the company, and for outside delivery they should be sent by registered or certified mail, or by a commercial overnight service.

Security for Information Processors and Communications Systems

One also must consider information security in terms of the information processor, such as a computer or communications system. Computer and information systems should be installed with the degree of security appropriate to their data contents and functions. A full program of monitoring and security procedures is needed to protect information systems and system products.

Computer tapes and disks consolidate large amounts of key information very compactly, and reconstruction of information could be very costly or impossible. Automated and manual procedures can be implemented to prevent and correct sloppy data input, and audit trails are important for fulfillment of business and government requirements. System documentation and system products—such as user manuals, codes, printouts, and documents—also need protection.

Computer security has not kept pace as computing power has moved from mainframes to desktops. Standard data processing controls frequently do not extend to the personal computers scattered throughout the office, in homes, and on the road. Standards for operation of personal computers and networks can address issues of proper use of software programs, memory, and functions.

Certain steps can be taken to prepare for recovery from a computer disaster—whether the disaster is accidental or intentional. Some computer systems can help reconstruct events in the case of inadvertent loss by an employee or by an intruder by creating an audit of information before and after changes, and the source and time of changes. If possible, and appropriate, a desktop computer's hard disk should be used to hold only programs, not to store data. Backups of data and software should be stored in a remote, safe place.

The computer disaster industry has been growing about 40 percent per year, according to Contingency Planning Research, a Jericho, New York, consulting firm. These vendors provide backup data storage and services, and some provide access to a hot site facility with compatible hardware in the event of damage or destruction to the company's own hardware. Because physical transportation of records to a remote records center could be a cumbersome, expensive, and not very secure procedure, some vendors have capabilities for electronic transmission of data to the center in such a way that meets a corporation's unique security requirements.

Electrical power problems can adversely affect equipment, and thus the information stored and processed on that equipment. In the event of a major power failure, an uninterruptible power system allows computers time to shut down in an orderly way for a soft landing, instead of crash landing. A backup power system allows business to continue normally without the primary power source. Protection against line noise and fluctuations also should be considered, as industry studies indicate that the majority of computer failures occur from brownouts, spikes, surges, and noise—not from major power losses.

Though the majority of computer security breaches occur from inside an organization, precautions against outside access may be needed. Use of systems and networks to transmit sensitive information should be avoided whenever possible. Special precautions may be needed for fax, voice, electronic, video, picture phone, and data transmissions, depending upon the sensitivity of the information. More and more communications systems are being introduced that prevent third-party intrusions, and data and digitized voice encryption may be desirable for transmission of highly sensitive information. Personal computer communications systems designed around government-approved encryption standards provide better security for faxes, electronic mail, file transfers, and keyboard conversations.

In some situations, different systems and networks are used to separate business functions such as finance, marketing, personnel, and purchasing. System interfaces can be designed to prevent or restrict access to systems, data files, read-write functions and other applications. An elaborate password system and assignment of security codes to types of data files and system applications also helps restrict access to authorized individuals with a need to know. For higher levels of security, a business might consider biometrics (the use of finger and voice prints), signatures, and eye patterns for system access. Gateway safeguards and port protection devices can lock out intruders or limit outside access to preauthorized phone numbers by using a call-back program.

Computer viruses and other mischief may result in the loss of hours, days, or weeks of work. The antivirus bells and whistles seem more exciting than other computer security measures, but viruses are less of a threat than operator error and broken pipes. Viral infection can be intentional or unintentional, but the virus threat can be reduced by following normal computer security procedures and a few specialized procedures, such as:

- Minimize connections to networks and phone lines.
- Partition or segment systems to establish write-protect areas of disks and to help prevent a spread through the system before detection.
- Allow only reputable off-the-shelf software on a system, or quarantine and test new products.
- Install monitoring software to inspect all files received via wire.
- Regularly check the size of a program to see if it has changed.

- Occasionally reload programs from a pure, original source.

Proper Destruction

The creators and users of sensitive or valuable records also frequently have the responsibility for their destruction. A records retention schedule is the formal authority for when records are to be destroyed according to legal and business requirements. A comprehensive retention schedule will also specify the disposition of outdated and superseded records, drafts, notes, and poor copies when they are no longer needed. The proliferation of photocopiers, computers, and optical disks makes it more difficult to ensure that all copies are disposed of at the proper time. The retention schedule must be applied to records in all media: paper, film, electronic, magnetic, optical disk, audio and video cassette, photo, slide, transparency, carbon ribbon, metal offset plates, and so on.

Proper disposition at the end of a sensitive or valuable record's life usually requires obliteration of the contents through mutilation or erasure. This type of destruction is an important substitute for tossing paper and microfilm records into the trash, where they become part of the public domain and accessible to the competition, computer hackers, and others. Erasure is used most frequently for dictation, audio, and video tapes, as well as electronic and magnetic media.

A lesson to be learned from Oliver North regarding electronic messaging and computer data systems: when messages and data are supposedly erased, they in fact may continue to exist on disk or on a network's file server, and other electronic "paper trails" and actual paper documents also may exist. Various file security programs and programs that really do erase all traces of a file may be used to ensure thorough destruction when appropriate.

Thanks in part to the Watergate scandal and the Iran-contra affair, the shredder equipment and services industry is growing. Some companies place shredders at the point of use, or protect records in security envelopes or locked containers until time for destruction in a central service area. A vendor that offers destruction services from a mobile shredding unit will eliminate any risks during transportation of the records to a vendor's facility for destruction. Every commercial service should sign an agreement to protect records until destruction and should be able to provide a certificate of destruction.

Shredder equipment comes in all sizes, models, and costs to meet different requirements for capacity, speed, media size and type, shred size, and even baling capabilities. Some models handle more than just paper—including ring binders and boxes—and other models process only specific media. Paper shredders start as low as $300 for a desktop model and go to over $100,000 for a free-standing, high-security model.

The 1979 Iranian hostage crisis began changing attitudes about shred size. Iranians were able to reconstruct more than half of the classified documents shredded into 1/4-inch strips according to State Department standards. The standard, straight-cut shredder is making way for confetti and disintegrator shredders, which continue to cut paper until it is small enough to fall through a screen. The disintegrator is now required for most Department of Defense records, including those in the possession of government contractors.

INFORMATION RELEASES TO OTHERS

There are occasions when it is appropriate or necessary to release valuable or sensitive information to suppliers, customers, other businesses, the litigants, the government, and other parties. A business will need to show due care when releasing information for such legitimate purposes.

Handling Requests for Information

After a company's sensitive and valuable information has been clearly identified and marked, new considerations come into play in the determination of when disclosure is appropriate and what protective measures need to be taken if the information is released. Clear guidelines are needed for proper information disclosure practices. Information releases may be initiated by:

- the company
- requests from others
- legal and statutory obligations to provide information

Disclosure of valuable and sensitive information normally is accompanied by appropriate restrictions to protect the best interests of the company. Just as a nondisclosure agreement is common for company insiders (employees, temporaries, and consultants), so is it also used when information is shared with outsiders (government agencies, suppliers, manufacturers, and other parties). When sensitive information is provided orally, there should be a written confirmation to the recipient to reaffirm that the information is sensitive and governed by a signed confidentiality agreement.

Very large companies can afford to hire a company proprietary information coordinator to review all proposed information releases. If unable to appoint a single expert, a business could rely on a list of resource people available to review specific types of information releases:

- The marketing department may handle releases to government agencies and foreign countries.

- An operations manager may review proposed releases of proprietary product information.

- The legal department should handle all disclosures related to legal matters.

- A human resources manager may handle requests for current and former employee information.

- The public relations staff may handle press relations, public speaking engagements, and publications.

The individual reviewing an information request should consider the nature of the material, its intended use, and the potential for further distribution. Is there a need to know, and will the information requested in fact meet the stated need? A decision to release information may rest solely on a court or regulatory requirement to provide the information or to prohibit its disclosure. Generally, information should not be released if an equivalent is available from commercial or public sources, if it will aid someone intent on fraud, or if it will have other adverse effects on the company or others. Consideration also must be given to whether or not the information requested is the property of others and is covered by a nondisclosure agreement, privacy laws, or other protective obligations.

Licensing should be considered for information that was costly to develop or has intrinsic value. If release of the information would involve a great deal of effort and cost, it might be appropriate to require payment above and beyond printing costs. A prime candidate for licensing or fees is technical information such as software and any related documentation. Additional considerations in the determination of software release might be what—if any—technical support will be required, and any plans for an updated version.

Employee Information

A business has an obligation to prevent improper circulation of employee information within its organization, and to prevent unauthorized disclosure to outside parties. Under the federal Privacy Act, state statutes, and collective bargaining agreements, employees have a right to know what records are created and maintained about them, who has access to those records, and how the information is used. The employee's right to inspect the information and to submit corrections should be clearly communicated on a regular basis.

Record-keeping requirements usually specify guidelines for access to personal information. A current or former employee, as well as a job applicant, usually submits a written request to ensure proper identification and provision of the matching file. Other access within an organization is normally restricted to those with a legitimate need to know, such as human resources personnel and the employee's supervisor. Procedures established for routine use of employee information should be documented so that a record of such disclosures may be reconstructed without the necessity for a separate, formal procedure for each disclosure.

Specific regulations or collective bargaining agreements specify the types of records open to access by an employee. These records normally are those used to determine the employee's qualifications for employment, promotion, transfer, termination, compensation, and disciplinary action. Some states allow exclusion of certain documents from disclosure to an employee, such as letters of reference, medical records, or records of any criminal investigation.

Authorization to release information to an outside party normally is required from current or former employees and from job applicants. Employee information also may be disclosed in the following circumstances:

- in response to requests to verify directory-type information, such as the fact of employment, dates of employment, job title, and job site location
- to a proper law enforcement authority when the company believes an employee is engaged in illegal or other threatening activities
- pursuant to a federal, state, or local compulsory reporting statute or regulation
- in response to an administrative summons or judicial order, including search warrant or subpoena

- to a collective bargaining unit pursuant to the contract
- to a company's agent or contractor when the information is necessary to perform its contracted function
- to a physician for the purpose of informing an employee of a medical problem

Suppliers, Manufacturers, and Other Businesses

A business typically discloses sensitive or valuable information to another business in a request for proposal, a proposal, a joint project, and when contracting with another party for a product or service. Such information sharing occurs when it is to the mutual benefit of both parties.

When developing a request for proposal or a proposal, consideration should be given to the extent to which it may become necessary to furnish valuable information to the other party in order to complete the project. Any such situation should include the appropriate nondisclosure agreements, and assurances may also be needed that the company retains certain rights to any work products as a result of the contract.

Common today among vendors of hardware, software, and communications are requests for information from other manufacturers or suppliers to assess interface capabilities or feasibility of their own developments. Many of these requests are driven by competitive intentions, but some are not. Occasionally, industry regulations obligate a company to furnish certain information. For example, telecommunications companies must furnish information about voice and data transmission services under certain circumstances. However, a company may apply protective agreements or may take steps to avoid disclosure of information that will aid the competition or make it more difficult for the company to compete. Information requests from potential competitors should be handled with caution, protecting valuable information while remaining in compliance with applicable laws and regulations.

In the Public Domain

There are a number of situations in which business information is disclosed in such a way that it becomes part of the public domain. A business needs to be aware of what information is provided to such sources—voluntarily or as a legal obligation—and must take the precautions necessary to prevent disclosure of inappropriate information wherever possible. Plans for trade shows, articles, research papers, speeches, books, and other activities proposed by technical people and management should be reviewed by a proprietary information coordinator or other appropriate management personnel. Business and financial news media reporters should be referred to public relations.

Government investigations and legal proceedings also put sensitive and valuable information at risk. Congressional hearings on a product, service, or practice are subject to the Freedom of Information Act. The discovery process of legal proceedings can place records directly into the hands of a competitor, and court records generally are a matter of public record. A company may appeal to the court for special consideration in the handling of proprietary information and the sealing of court proceedings and records, but a movement is on today to make that more difficult.

Every business must file records with federal, state, and local governments. A large number of businesses also must submit information to state and federal government agencies, such as OSHA and the EPA. Government contractors also have information that is subject to public disclosure requirements, and regulated businesses must file documents with regulatory commissions. Even the very attempt to protect one's property through patent and copyright registrations may result in government records that are open to the public.

A business needs to tailor its government filings to minimize release of sensitive information. The Freedom of Information Act, a law requiring public disclosure of federal agencies' records and information, allows certain exceptions for government-classified, trade secret or private information. Protective agreements should be used when valuable information is provided. A business may have to defend its desire for confidentiality when the parties involved move to have the information declared nonproprietary in order to copy it or release it to others. If the business fails to justify confidentiality, a document will probably need to remain nonproprietary in all other business and legal situations.

Records Vital to a Business

Every business has records that are essential to its operations and to its very existence. In today's highly competitive environment, it is critical that a company be able to continue operations throughout an emergency situation, and be able to resume critical business functions in an orderly and timely manner after a manmade or natural disaster. Action taken to preserve the ability to continue business operations could prove to be a company's salvation in the event of a disaster.

The importance of records protection is most fully understood and appreciated by those who have experienced losses from a fire, tornado, earthquake, or computer disaster. Disaster victims, more capable of clearly visualizing the real and potential losses from these unexpected emergencies, have faced the difficult task of producing the documentation necessary to receive public and private relief.

There are ethical and legal obligations to maintain the viability of a business. It is good business sense to have an emergency plan for protection of records that document legal identity, rights, and obligations. Aside from the simple motive to stay in business, outside pressures from shareholders, regulatory agencies, insurance carriers, and accounting firms may compel development of a disaster plan.

A VITAL RECORDS SCHEDULE

In very simple terms, records vital to a business are those records necessary during the emergency conditions and those records required to fulfill its obligations, to retain its rights, and to go about its business. They are records essential to the continuation or resumption of business activities as quickly as possible in the event of a loss.

Vital records cannot be replaced easily, or are impossible to replace. They are necessary for business operations to continue with the least degree of financial loss or in convenience. They also are the records critical to the provision of products and services—the livelihood of a business. Without certain records, a company is incapable of accomplishing its intended activities and pursuing its interests.

In the strictest sense, vital records are the documents that preserve the legal status and existence of the organization, such as articles of incorporation, by-laws, minute books, stock certificates, and shareowner information. They also are records that protect and provide direct evidence of legal rights and privileges, assets, and incurred obligations.

Certain vital records substantiate important relationships between the company and others. They identify the rights and obligations of the company, employees and their dependents, stockholders and their heirs, clients or customers, creditors, suppliers, bondholders, the government, and the general public. Such vital records also ensure the capability to meet commitments and obligations to employees, customers, and others.

The records associated with critical business functions are usually considered vital records. Vital financial records include those that show the status of a company's assets and liabilities. They provide evidence of ownership in the form of negotiable documents and records of property and fixed assets. They protect the equity of the owners and company obligations in the form of accounts payable, payroll, taxes, and other similar records.

Vital records are those required to substantiate a claim or payment. Records necessary to prevent income losses include sales agreements, receivables, and other documents required to recover monies due. They are also records and information critical to operations, manufacturing, research and development, provision of services, and other means of earning income.

Vital data and documents include those that fulfill the information requirements of disaster conditions and operations during the emergency and throughout the recovery phase, which may be different from the information requirements of normal business conditions. Such records provide the capability to reconstruct company operations within a reasonable time period at an equitable cost. Their reconstruction or reproduction after a disaster would be too costly in terms of dollars and time, and would adversely delay the restoration process. Records are needed for various specific disaster and restoration tasks:

• filing insurance claims
• rebuilding facilities
• resuming product manufacturing or data processing operations
• developing new business

Vital records and information may be in the form of paper, microform, electronic or magnetic data, photographs, or other media. Typically, from 2 to 10 percent of a company's records are vital to a business. The big question is, which 2 or 10 percent? The type of industry, regulatory requirements, methods of operation, the nature of its products and services, and the marketplace will help determine which records are vital to a business. Every business will designate as vital its records documenting legal and financial status, liabilities, what is owed the company and what the company owes, the value of owned property, the locations and amounts of cash and securities, inventory on hand, and so forth. Examples of records and information that may be considered vital to the continuation of business are:

• accident reports
• articles of incorporation and other corporate records
• assets inventories, deeds, and titles
• contracts and agreements
• costing records
• customer lists
• disaster plan
• engineering specifications
• forms
• financial registers, statements, and ledgers
• insurance records
• manufacturing process
• mineral rights, rights of way, and easements
• patent, trademark, and service mark records
• payroll and pension records
• performance standards and test results

- policies and practices
- records retention documentation
- research and development
- stock and dividend payments
- tax obligations and payments

A vital records schedule is a tool to identify vital records and to establish proper protection and salvage methods and practices. The schedule is developed by a review of an inventory of the company's records and information. After elimination of the records that can be reconstructed from other records and those that will not be necessary during or after an emergency, the nature and value of records is then considered.

Records associated with critical business functions typically are selected for protection. Those critical business functions are emergency conditions, the time period immediately after the emergency, the recovery phase, and finally, the resumption of normal business conditions. The extent to which loss of a record would delay or prevent critical business activities must be considered. The relative difficulty and expense involved in replacement or reconstruction of records required during and after the emergency are also considerations. Top priority are those records necessary for immediate business operations. Second priority are those necessary for operations within the first month, but not immediately. Third priority are those needed for business and legal applications after thirty days.

Identification of vital records is a matter of interest throughout the organization. This responsibility should not be assigned to a single department. The chief executive officer or president of a company should create a task force or committee made up of representatives from key functional areas to perform this task. Business functions to be represented in such an effort include:

- auditing
- data processing
- finance
- legal
- marketing
- operations or manufacturing
- records management

- security

Careful selection will limit protection to only those records deemed essential to planned purposes. The schedule must remain current and accurate at all times. An annual review of the schedule is recommended to make any adjustments as necessary to accommodate any new records groups or changes in the business situation.

As part of the vital record identification process, the following information should be noted:

- the media and location of the original record
- the reason for protection as a vital record (this may be useful later if the situation changes)
- whether or not the record is regularly audited
- the record's historical value, if any
- the proposed protection method
- the appropriate disposition of the record when the record is superseded by an updated version or when the vital retention expires
- the record's normal length of retention
- the destruction method to use when the overall retention period expires

A prioritization of records to be salvaged will help reduce delays and expenses in recovery. After selection of vital records, the committee determines the length of time these records should be protected as vital. A record's function and the frequency of updates help determine how frequently a vital record is transferred into and out of protection.

Some records are retained for the life of the corporation and remain vital for that entire time period, such as charters of incorporation, by-laws, and minutes from board of directors meetings. Other records to be protected for an extended period of time are those representing legal obligations to employees, stockholders, creditors, and others. A large portion of vital records are replaced on a scheduled basis as the information is routinely updated. When a list of current stockholders or customers is updated, for example, the superseded list is no longer considered vital. Accounts receivable records are constantly changing, so only the most current records would be considered vital. Vital record rotation frequencies may be annual, quarterly, monthly, weekly, or daily.

A vital records schedule also should indicate what to do with any superseded copy. Some records need to be retained for periods longer than their vital record status, especially if they are litigation records, historical records, or other records to meet business and financial needs. At the end of the vital protection period, the record must be returned to another records storage system for the duration of its full retention period as prescribed by the company's records retention schedule.

THE VITAL RECORDS PROGRAM

The ultimate purpose of any disaster program is to position an organization so as to assure that operations, employees, and assets effectively survive the impact of a disastrous event. The preservation of vital records is a key to that success, and the vital records program should be a key element of a corporate-wide disaster plan. Though it is advisable to have an overall disaster plan, it is possible to develop a vital records program in the absence of one.

A well-conceived disaster plan and vital records program can be economical in its development, maintenance, and implementation by including elements of risk analysis, prevention and protection; preparedness; crisis management; and salvage and recovery. Close coordination with an existing information security and risk management program will respond to many vital records protection requirements.

Program development is best accomplished by a team of information users and subject experts from throughout the organization. Input and coordination are needed from key functional areas of the business, including:

- auditing
- communications
- customer service
- facility management
- finance
- human resources
- legal
- management information systems
- marketing
- operations and production
- purchasing and inventory
- records and information management

- risk management and insurance
- security
- transportation

Each representative can offer valuable contributions to the tasks of risk analysis, disaster prevention, emergency preparedness, and recovery. Team members participate in the development of the criteria, strategies, guidelines, and resources necessary for disaster planning and implementation activities. They recommend appropriate facilities, equipment, supplies, and practices to reduce losses in the event of a disaster. The team also determines what individuals should constitute a disaster team to coordinate emergency activities. The vital records program should be in writing and should be kept current. It must be readily available to the designated disaster team during emergency conditions.

Administration of the vital records program should be the responsibility of the records and information manager. This individual chairs the vital records program team and the vital records schedule development team, and coordinates the vital records program with the corporate disaster plan. The records manager oversees vital records facilities and services, develops standards and practices, inventories vital records on a regular basis, and ensures that vital records remain in usable condition and remain available for prompt retrieval when they are needed.

Risk Analysis

Risk analysis is a strategic approach to program development that promotes its cost-effectiveness. The scope of a program is determined by a number of factors, including the type and degree of potential threats and risks to records and information. The vital records program team assesses the likelihood of various natural and manmade disasters, the probabilities of loss or damage to documents and data, and the consequences of that damage or loss.

Fire is a common information security threat, the cause of nine in ten data losses. The degree of risk from natural disasters depends on the geographic location of a business, and some business sites are more susceptible to electrical power problems than others. Facilities, equipment, and communications and computer systems also may pose physical threats and security problems for recorded information.

After identification of areas of calculated risk, the team determines what is most at risk and what truly merits full protection. Priorities are established for the time and resources necessary for program development, prevention, protection, and recovery. Insurance adjusters may be of assistance in establishing priorities by providing information on repair and recovery costs, time periods necessary for such repairs and recovery procedures, what documentation is required, and the extent and limits of the coverage that is currently in effect or is available.

Costs involved in a disaster plan may include planning, facility modifications for better environmental and security controls, services, equipment, supplies, backup systems, retrieval, and record reproduction. The costs are simply an investment in the company's future, and could become negligible when compared to losses in the absence of a program. In addition, a business with a well-structured disaster recovery plan may be eligible for a price break on its insurance.

Risk analysis balances the costs of re-creation of records versus protection. It balances the costs of preservation through backup systems or insurance versus the costs of loss prevention through facility modifications. Risk analysis also balances the costs of recovery in the form of salvage, restoration, and reproduction against the costs of re-creation of information lost or the complete loss of information.

Prevention and Protection

The prevention and protection phase of a vital records program is the development of practices and methods to reduce the probability and the consequences of risks. The vital records schedule identifies the records to be protected and the suggested methods of protection. The final determination of prevention and protection methods is based on an analysis of the risks and costs. The costs of prevention and protection must be weighed against the costs of recovery, re-creation, and loss of records and information.

A combination of strategies may be used to protect and preserve vital records in various media, as described later in this chapter. Prevention efforts identify hazards, risks, and security problems in all facilities. The vital records team makes recommendations to prevent or reduce damage or loss, and prioritizes those recommendations for economical implementation as funds become available.

Prevention and protection procedures are established to ensure appropriate use of records in daily operations and to ensure that the records will be readily available during the emergency situation, immediately after the crisis for the recovery phase, and for resumption of normal business operations.

Preparedness

Preparedness measures provide for a quick, rational response to actual emergency situations and for the prevention of escalation of the damages. The vital records schedule, a key document resource for the preparedness aspect of a program, identifies the records being protected from loss and the backup systems in place.

Backup information systems will include data, hardware, and hot site facilities required to retrieve and process recorded information. Companies are more likely to have computer data backups, but they do not always consider system and hardware backups, and they frequently neglect protection of film and paper records. Microfilm and computer records will be useless in an emergency that destroys the computer facility, computer equipment, and microfilm readers and printers.

The preparedness element of the program also details disaster condition operating and recovery procedures, outlines salvage methods, and lists resources that may be necessary during and after the emergency. Responsibilities of individuals and their authority are clearly spelled out and available on a moment's notice, along with emergency numbers, floor plans, and recovery operations guidelines for each facility.

The list of resources for emergency situations and for salvage and recovery activities must be kept current. Many companies secure agreements with these companies in anticipation of any need. For example, a growing number of businesses are signing on with computer disaster service companies. The list of available resources may include:

- owned or leased facilities that would be available for emergency and recovery operations and storage
- owned or leased facilities and equipment for computer operations
- salvage and recovery services, such as computer data disaster centers, film reprocessing centers, vacuum- or freeze-drying facilities, refrigerated trucks and facilities, transportation companies
- sources for salvage and recovery equipment and supplies (plastic sheeting and trash bags, dehumidifiers, fans, portable pumps and generators, heavy-duty extension cords, plastic crates, forklifts, etc.)
- sources for replacement of damaged or lost equipment and supplies
- technical experts (contractors, exterminators, data processing technicians)
- insurance agents

Scheduled and unscheduled audits of the vital records disaster plan determine the plan's feasibility and the level of preparedness for quality operations under extraordinary conditions. An audit will identify any inadequacies and any need to update controls and protection methods to keep up with changing business needs and changing information systems and technologies.

An audit may test the timely availability of records, and transfers of records into and out of vital records protection. A common test is to give the disaster team a set of information needs that the company would have after a disaster. The team must demonstrate how the company would re-create or retrieve the information after an emergency in order to do any of the following:

- continue paying employees and making proper deductions
- prepare a current inventory of all corporate assets
- send new shipping instructions to vendors with outstanding orders
- prepare an insurance claim for all or part of a facility and its contents
- resume production or provision of services in a certain area

Crisis Management

Emergency agencies and personnel to be called immediately when a disaster occurs should be identified in the vital records plan. While the fire department or other emergency services are busy with the crisis situation, the vital records disaster team can begin identification of needed vital records and their locations.

Salvage and Recovery

After the air clears and the water subsides, the disaster team inventories damaged records and refers to the written plan and procedures for follow-up action. Priorities for salvage and salvage methods are determined for an action plan.

Undamaged records may need to be temporarily removed to prevent damage from any facility clean-up activities. Damaged records must be moved to a work area for drying or repair procedures. Procedures may differ for preparation and handling of paper records, photographic materials, microforms, magnetic or electronic tapes, and other record forms.

Special cleaning methods may be needed to remove contaminants and other foreign particles deposited by storm drains, pipes, or a flood. Contaminants are especially damaging to microforms. Special procedures are necessary to salvage water damage to tapes and photo materials. Service centers and mobile units are available to vacuum-dry or freeze-dry paper records. Vacuum drying is faster than freeze-drying, but freeze-drying is best when any delay in drying could result in damage from mold and fungus growth.

PROTECTION AGAINST THREATS TO VITAL RECORDS

Threats to the security of records and information are thoroughly discussed in Chapter 7, "Sensitive and Valuable Records and Information." Methods to protect vital records include many of those discussed in Chapter 8, "Records and Information Security," but additional measures are necessary to prepare for and recover from a disastrous event.

Only a conscious, planned effort can protect vital business information from any conceivable hazard. Methods used to protect vital records will vary according to usage patterns, the nature of the information, and the medium on which the information is recorded. The value of a record as it relates to revenues, services, products, or liabilities determines the degree to which the record should be protected. How records are protected may be as simple and inexpensive as returning records to their storage cabinets to reduce or prevent possible water damage. They may be as expensive as creating a microfilm security copy of documents for storage in an off-site vault with special environmental and security controls.

Record Medium

In terms of vital records, the choice of information carrier is a factor deserving of special attention. The physical qualities of an information carrier determine its susceptibility to damage or loss caused by adverse environmental conditions, use, and aging.

Risks and costs are lowest when protective measures begin at the time the record is created and the medium is chosen. The protection and preservation of paper and microform records will remain crucial issues for decades to come for mature corporations and for companies aspiring to grow old. Certain vital records must be maintained in their original paper form to retain their value, such as executed contracts, deeds, and titles.

Paper and microform are recommended for vital records that need to be retained for more than one year and that must be immediately accessible in an emergency. Except for optical disk, computer information systems normally should not be relied on for permanent or long-term storage and security. If the computer medium is selected, the vital records task force must handle these tasks:

* identify a backup computer
* identify and synchronize associated programs, systems software and hardware required to recover the information
* provide for backups to be updated on a regular basis

Security Copying and Dispersal

A common method of protecting a vital record is to physically segregate duplicate copies of the record. In large corporations, this activity often is routine; small businesses are much more vulnerable when they store all records in a single facility. A vital record may be duplicated in the same or a different medium. The copies may be sent to other company locations that are considered relatively safe from disaster, or they are sent far enough away so as not to be affected by a disaster at another location. Any equipment necessary to retrieve, read, and reproduce nonpaper information must be readily available in the event of a disaster.

Dispersal is the least expensive preservation method. It is based on the assumption that the same disaster is not likely to strike all locations at the same time. Protection is considered adequate when duplicates are sent to at least three well-separated facilities. Using a built-in or existing dispersal method, duplicate records are automatically distributed to other departments and locations through normal business activities. These records are retained unaltered at those locations until they are superseded by an updated copy or until their retention period ends and they are destroyed.

Caution should be used when relying on duplicate records kept on file by a government agency or other organization. Quick retrieval of a duplicate from a government agency is highly unlikely. If a business depends on a creditor to maintain a duplicate record of its liabilities, it must remember that the creditor's interests are different from its own. When relying on an accounting or law firm for backup duplicate copies, the company should ensure that the firm retains the records for as long as the company deems necessary. There also is the possibility that the firm could be a victim of the same disaster that hits the company's own facility.

A planned dispersal is less risky than a built-in dispersal. It offers control over any changes in procedures, and it does not assume that someone else is keeping a copy. In planned dispersal, a duplicate is made at the time of record creation expressly for security purposes. This duplicate is stored at another location for normal use and reference, and the original is sent to a vital records center. If it is not necessary to retain the original, a microform copy for the vital records center will reduce storage space requirements and expense. One copy of computer tapes and diskettes should be stored off site, and another copy should be stored in fire and water resistant containers and equipment on site.

On-site Protection

On-site records protection may be accomplished by fire- and water-resistant space, storage equipment, and record containers. Records maintained inside closed cabinets that are six inches up from the floor will have less water damage than those outside of the cabinet or those immediately next to the floor. Mobile file units should be closed when not in use to retard the spread of fire. Polyethylene or metal containers for tapes and computer media, and insulated file cabinets and equipment, can minimize damage from flame and water.

Fire-resistant file cabinets are useful for records that would require substantial expenditures of time or money for their reconstruction, but they are not adequate for full protection of vital records. Vaults on site are best for short-term storage of vital records that are updated or changed frequently, and the copies should be sent off site on a regular basis for best protection of the information. Vaults are a capital expense and should be treated as such: store only vital records in them—not office supplies—and keep the doors closed.

Computer records also are vulnerable to environmental and human threats. Backup data and systems must be provided for, and unauthorized access to computers must be prevented.

Vital Records Center

A vital records center is designed to meet the objectives of segregation and preservation. As a separate facility dedicated to the preservation of its contents, the vital records center normally houses original records. Duplicate records generally are stored elsewhere for use as a working copy or a backup if needed. More than one security copy of an active record may be needed in other locations.

A vital records center may be a company's own facility, or it may be a commercial facility. In either case, it must be located away from normal operations, preferably in another city. Vital records from east coast operations are best stored in a midwestern or western state facility, and vice versa. A word of caution for multistate companies: do not attempt to reduce storage and protection costs by consolidating records from a number of locations into one facility. A disaster at that facility could truly be disastrous to the entire company.

A vital records center has security and environmental conditions different from those of the standard records center. Proper environmental conditions are especially important for records with a long retention period. Controls must be in place to prevent damage from insects, rodents, ultraviolet light, pollutants, and water and power failures. The condition of records should be periodically checked and storage conditions adjusted as appropriate. Security at a vital records center must be tighter than normal, and its fire-fighting system should not be dependent on a public water supply.

Commercial facilities that provide vital records security and storage are in a large number of cities across the country, and more and more vendors are specializing in computer data services. For all but the largest businesses, it is most economical to use a commercial facility. These facilities often are in unpopulated areas, and many are located underground or in converted mines to take advantage of previous natural or manmade excavations and natural temperature and humidity controls. Records may be most vulnerable while in transit to a center, so backup copies should be safeguarded until the records arrive safely at the center.

Usage and Disposition

Vital records must be organized and stored so as to be readily accessible in the event of an emergency. Their use should be restricted to a list of authorized users under certain conditions. A vital record copy should be recalled for use in other than an emergency situation only if all other copies are unavailable. If possible and appropriate, a copy should be made in order to avoid damage or loss in transit or during use. Special procedures to transmit or ship vital records must be established for the occasion when it is necessary to do so for normal operations, during an emergency, and for recovery operations. The equipment necessary to use microforms and computer records also must be readily available.

10

Records Retention and Disposition

A typical executive, tax manager, or corporate attorney would sleep better at night knowing that the company is documenting every business transaction or activity, and is maintaining those records forever. But storage of the billions of new documents that are created every year is simply not practical in terms of costs and operational efficiencies. Few businesses can afford to store and properly preserve all records that they receive and generate for extended periods of time. Records storage costs mount up in terms of space, equipment, supplies, personnel, and information security and preservation.

The traditional tendency to keep records permanently stems primarily from a fear of being sued and a reluctance to make decisions. Keeping records is easier than having to determine what to destroy and when. But the evidence is piling up against keeping everything. Records retained longer than required are being subpoenaed, adding unnecessary records to the already burdensome document review and production process. Worse yet, the content of records may be taken out of context, misinterpreted, and used against their owners by an opposing party.

MANAGING VOLUMES OF RECORDS

At one time or another, every business faces the dilemma of having to decide what records to keep and what records to destroy. Studies show that typically more than 80 percent of the records filed are never referred to again, and that 40 percent are completely without value. But which

Figure 10.1
A Delicate Balance

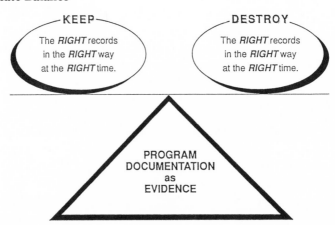

records have real value, and which have no value at all? What records lose their value after a period of time, and how long is that interval?

It would be irresponsible for a company to be overzealous by clearing out boxes of records without appropriate guidelines. A systematic approach to records destruction is especially important in companies likely to be involved in litigation or government investigation. Any haphazard or adhoc approach could be construed as selective destruction and thus have negative consequences.

A records retention and disposition program helps a business regain control over the proliferation of its records and information. The program maintains that delicate balance of having enough of the right records and not having too many records. Figure 10.1 illustrates this delicate balance, which rests on program documentation as evidence.

A records retention program, the very heart of records and information management, identifies:

- valuable and necessary records to be retained to meet business and legal requirements
- the appropriate media for various records
- official record copies versus duplicate copies
- when it is best to convert records from one medium to another
- when it is more economical to transfer records to a less costly storage facility
- when it is appropriate to finally dispose of the records

Though a retention program may be costly to develop and administer in terms of human and capital resources, the costs of not having a systematic program in place are greater. Aside from the costs to manage unnecessary records, the legal justifications for a records retention and disposition program are quite persuasive. Certain records must be maintained in order to comply with the law or to show compliance with the law. If business does not follow the rules—including maintenance of records to show its compliance with the rules—it may lose its legal rights or be subject to civil or criminal charges and penalties, or to adverse inferences. Other records no longer necessary are destroyed to prevent unnecessary legal costs and liabilities. As awareness of the benefits of a records retention program grows, more and more attorneys are advising their clients to establish such a program.

A Retention Schedule

A retention schedule is a vehicle for conducting the activity of records retention and disposition in a systematic, rational manner. The development of a retention schedule forces management to make some hard decisions based on long-term business needs and legal requirements. The ultimate objective of a retention schedule is to meet business needs and legal requirements, and to destroy records at the earliest possible time in the best interests of the business.

In its purest form, a schedule identifies what records are to be maintained, in what form(s), and for how long. A more advanced retention schedule includes instructions for disposition other than destruction, such as conversion to another medium or transfer to another location. As a management tool, the schedule not only controls the volume of records, but also organizes the fewer remaining records for better access, and may be used to develop projections of future record-keeping resource requirements.

The retention schedule of ForwardThink Corporation covers records in all media. The schedule is based on a subject listing of its records and the appropriate retention requirements for each group of records. Some records groups have instructions for when inactive records are to be transferred to the records storage facility, or when they are to be microfilmed and what to do with the original paper record. The schedule also prescribes frequencies and methods of backing up computer records and transferring the backups to the computer data security center. Upon expiration of the final retention period for a group of records, those records are retrieved in all of their various forms and destroyed by trashing, shredding, and computer record deletion procedures.

A retention schedule must apply to all records that have a real or potential impact on the business, its employees and customers, government relations, court proceedings, and the general public. This includes paper and computer records, microforms, audio and video tapes, photographs, and so forth. But the proliferation of photocopiers, computers, and other office technologies makes it more difficult to administer a retention program. If a retention and disposition program is not applied to all records, a court of law may question the systematic destruction of records according to an established schedule when records that should have been destroyed continue to be available through a computer, microform, paper, or other record form.

At The House of Good Intentions, the retention schedule for paper and microfilm records is not coordinated with the MIS department's procedures for computer records. As a result, COM and paper printouts of computer data are not routinely destroyed when the original computer data is deleted, and computer records continue to exist when the related paper and microfilm records are destroyed according to their retention schedule. In some cases, a file on a computer diskette is deleted under the assumption that a paper or microfilm copy is being retained, when in fact it is not. If the integrity of the record retention program of The House of Good Intentions were ever to come under scrutiny in court, the company's inability to apply the same retention and destruction procedures to all records in all media could jeopardize any claim of a systematic records destruction program.

Duplicate records also must be controlled to reduce storage and handling costs and to preserve the integrity of a systematic retention program. A duplicate record normally has the same legal significance as an original under the rules of evidence, so it is deserving of the same attention as that given to designated record copies. A guideline instructing a specific retention period for duplicate records that clearly spells out acceptable exceptions will help control them. A word of caution about duplicate records: a duplicate record is considered a designated record copy when it has significant marginal notes, and should be retained for the full applicable retention period.

Taking a hard line on duplicate records, ForwardThink Corporation has established this policy: "Duplicate records must be destroyed within one year from their creation. Exceptions are authorized by the office of records and information management. Exceptions to this duplicate records destruction policy are permitted for duplicate copies in these records groups: budgets (2 years); accounts receivable (3 years); paper copies of general ledger records that are on microfilm (4 years); employee training records in field offices (3 years)."

All other records not described in a retention schedule are considered nonessential, and should be disposed of immediately or as soon as they are no longer in use.

RETENTION AND DISPOSITION DECISIONS

The creation and maintenance of records is compelled by business needs and a number of considerations that originate from other sources. When taken one step further, these needs and requirements are used to help determine when those records have served their useful purpose(s) within a more systematic approach to record-keeping.

A retention schedule is a blend of user needs, stated legal requirements, and additional legal considerations. The legal considerations are based on the amount of risk the business is willing to assume, interpretation of intent of the law, contractual terms, statutes of limitations, and litigation strategies. The final retention decision for each records group is based on the relative value of a record group as it affects these requirements. Value is assessed according to current or anticipated uses of the records category by the business, the government, or a court of law.

Business Needs

Every business has its own needs for records and information. Records are necessary for planning, resources management, and proper management of daily activities and business transactions. If a vital records schedule exists, some of the work already has been done regarding records transfers and disposition of superseded vital records. Interviews of records creators and users also help determine business needs in the basic functional areas, including:

• administration

- corporate history
- finance
- human resources
- manufacturing and production
- marketing, sales, and customer relations
- research and development
- securities and shareholder relations
- strategic planning
- tax and legal matters

Records creators and users also may be consulted on suggested record forms, but the final decision should be based on factors such as legal and retention requirements. Records users throughout departments will have a good idea of how long individual records groups should be maintained. They also know when a record becomes inactive and ready for transfer to a lower-cost records center. The decision to transfer inactive records to another location is strictly a business decision and is not based on any legal requirement.

Legal Record-Keeping Requirements

Compliance with the law regarding record retention is not as difficult as it might seem. Essentially, laws tend to reflect good business practices. As an example, every business normally creates and maintains many of the financial records that are needed for tax returns in order to meet its own needs. A retention program simply makes sure that these records are protected and maintained for the appropriate period of time to meet legal requirements.

In recognition of the fact that telephone companies maintain records in the normal course of business, the FCC eliminated hundreds of its record-keeping requirements, including record retention requirements. The commission now requires those companies to develop their own retention schedules.

Government regulations do exist that deviate from generally accepted business practices. These differences between government and business needs primarily occur in situations where the public interest is not yet fully defined, or where government purposes for the records differ from those of business. For example, the government requires for medical records of employees exposed to hazardous substances a much longer retention period than a business normally would, because the government's interest is in monitoring problems that may not develop for many years.

Government requirements may contain clearly stated record-keeping instructions, implied requirements, instructions that are confusing or that contradict other record-keeping requirements, or no instructions at all. State requirements may exist where federal requirements do not, or they may be different from federal requirements.

A federal requirement specifies that records of employee injuries should be maintained for five years after the injury. However, state OSHA and worker compensation laws may have a different retention period, and may note special exceptions. A state might extend the time for an employee to file a worker compensation claim if there is a "reasonable excuse" for not filing within the designated time period.

More than half of the stated requirements to create or maintain records do not specify how long to retain those records. There are requirements that specify the acceptable form(s) of a record and the conditions under which each form is acceptable. A few government record-keeping requirements go so far as to specify storage conditions and information security methods. Many statutes and regulations do not specify any record-keeping requirements at all, but it would be in the best interest of a business to anticipate the implications of its record-keeping practices regarding rules of evidence and the demonstration of compliance.

There are certain records that may be affected by more than one law or regulation. For example, the same payroll records necessary to support tax claims also may be needed to show compliance with equal pay regulations. Or one regulatory agency may require that certain records be maintained for six months, while those same records may be needed for 18 months to satisfy Department of Justice requirements.

Not all of the thousands of federal, state, local, and foreign records retention requirements impact every business. Companies normally need to comply with those federal requirements applicable to every business and those related to their industries and individual business activities. Every location where the company is doing business, where it has a facility, property, or employees, or where it is incorporated, is subject to a number of state and local requirements. A business also needs to research other legal considerations, such as statutes of limitations and rules of evidence.

The TechTrack firm is doing business in 14 states. Research of federal and state requirements turned up 900 applicable record-keeping requirements.

A company must make an effort to be reasonably informed of the law and to stay current on the rapid changes in statutes, regulations, and case law, as they affect its record-keeping requirements. Most businesses already have some of that knowledge scattered throughout their organization. A safety manager is familiar with OSHA regulations, a human resources manager is aware of employment requirements, and a contracts administrator knows contract requirements. Centralizing this knowledge, confirming and updating it, and filling in the blanks can be a relatively simple task.

There is no single source to determine all federal, administrative agency, and state records requirements, so it is difficult to efficiently conduct a comprehensive research project. Hampering a thorough search are poor indexing of requirements and untimely or no publication of requirements. A number of publications are available that include suggested retention schedules for businesses, and many of them provide regular updates. However, a business will want to modify such schedules in consultation with legal counsel to meet its own needs.

Most corporate legal departments are reluctant to devote the time necessary for research and interpretation of the laws as they apply to business situations. Outside counsel often is used for this service. Legal counsel should review and approve the results of research done by anyone not formally trained in conducting legal research. Regardless of who does the research, it is important to make a reasonable attempt to find, interpret, and apply the law, and to update the research every year.

Contracts and Agreements

Legal requirements regarding record-keeping also may be found in contracts and agreements.

Records belonging to one party that are in the possession of another party frequently are covered by a contract of some sort. Hospitals and clinics, and law, accounting, and engineering firms may not modify, destroy, or turn over to a third party the records belonging to others without permission of the owner or a court-ordered subpoena.

Responsibility for the records of one company acquired by another normally will be covered by agreement. If this is not made clear in the agreement, the organization responsible for the debts and obligations of the acquired company normally will be responsible for the records.

Federal contractors have record-keeping requirements, as stated in various federal laws and regulations applicable to all contractors. They also may have additional requirements specifically stated in the contract.

The House of Good Intentions has a contract with the federal government. Regulations regarding federal contracts provide for records retention of three years after completion of the contract. Exceptions to this retention period are cost accounting and procurement records, to be retained for four years, and time cards, to be retained for two years. A review of the contract reveals that in addition, specific employee records must be retained for five years.

Statutes of Limitations

If no record retention requirement exists, the statute of limitations becomes an especially important legal consideration.

Most tax regulations do not state a record retention requirement. Retention decisions for tax-related records must factor in the limitation of assessment time period and the retention requirements applicable to those records that support a tax return, such as property, sales, and insurance records.

The federal limitation of assessment time period is three years after a return is filed or the tax becomes due. During this time, the IRS may assess or collect taxes or initiate legal proceedings. In addition, the taxpayer may demand a refund or a credit during this time. An exception to this limitation of assessment time period may be the extension of the time period to six years if the taxpayer mistakenly—or otherwise—understates the gross income by 25 percent or more.

Because most states use the federal tax return as the basis for their own income tax, a business will need to retain the federal return's records for as long as they are necessary to support the state income tax return.

Statutes of limitation, or limitations of actions, are found in federal and state statutes and regulations. A statute of limitations specifies the time period during which an organization or individual may sue or be sued after an event, and the time period during which a government agency may investigate or audit the matter. Statutes of limitations do not impose a legal requirement to retain records, but they are a legal consideration that must be part of the decision-making process when determining records retention. It is important to identify the relevant limitations of actions in every state in which a company does business, and when each statute of limitations time period begins.

Litigation strategies may be developed that result in a decision to retain a records group longer than business needs dictate, or longer than the government requires, in order to protect the company's interests within a statute of limitations. If a statute of limitations allows legal action within six years, and the business wants to retain the right and the opportunity to take action or to defend itself within this time period, it will consider maintaining related records for all or part of the statute of limitations, even when that time period is longer than other record-keeping requirements. (See Chapter 4, "A Day in Court," for litigation strategies as they relate to records retention decisions.)

Court Proceedings and Government Investigations

The greater the likelihood that a record will be produced for a court proceeding or government investigation, the more important it is that the selected form of the record be one that meets the applicable rules of evidence. Federal and state rules of evidence may speak to conditions under which original, duplicate, microform, and computer records are acceptable.

Certain forms of records are not yet clearly covered under rules of evidence, including optical disk, voice messaging, and electronic mail. Where new technologies are concerned, a business will need to anticipate future legal requirements or attempt to apply as well as possible existing requirements related to similar records forms.

The Uniform Photographic Copies of Business and Public Records as Evidence Act (UPA) allows duplicate records when the technology or process to produce that record can be shown to reproduce accurately an original record. This law also permits destruction of an original record. However, exceptions to the destruction of an original record after it has been duplicated are found in regulations that affect federal contractors, businesses holding the records of others, and other laws that require preservation of the original record.

The routine destruction of records that are relevant to any foreseeable or pending legal action or government investigation must be suspended as soon as the business is aware of the action. More information on the suspension of routine record destruction because of a legal, tax, or audit hold is found at the end of this chapter and in Chapter 4, "A Day in Court."

Finalizing Retention Decisions

When no legal considerations can be found for a records group, the best strategy may be to retain the records for three years. However, a retention period longer than three years might be necessary for historical, research and development, and other records that are critical to long-term business needs. This suggested three-year retention is based on the Uniform Preservation of Private Business Records Act and—with some exceptions—affects federal record-keeping requirements and the requirements of the handful of states that have adopted the law as of this writing.

Every decision to retain or not to retain a records group involves analysis of the costs, benefits, and risks involved. To provide a full and equitable analysis, attorneys may need to become educated on records management principles and the benefits of controlling large volumes of records for manageability, efficiencies, and cost savings. Retention decisions should be based on sound business practices and should allow for as much flexibility as possible within the existing legal, practical, and ethical constraints.

The final records retention schedule must be approved in writing by the departments responsible for individual records groups, by legal counsel, the tax administrator, and the records and information management manager. Written approvals of the final retention schedule will demonstrate both systematic development of the retention schedule and company-wide support of the program.

The selected retention periods are not cast in concrete. Records categories, legal considerations, and business activities will change over time, but any changes in the retention schedule must not be treated casually. Changes must be justified and approved by the appropriate personnel and by legal counsel, and the process must be fully documented.

Once it is determined how long records are to be maintained, efforts must be made to preserve those records for their full retention period. Knowing how long a record will be retained becomes a major factor to consider when selecting the record's medium. All records designated for retention must be protected from damage or loss. This includes making sure that computer data, hardware, software, and indexing are preserved so as to be able to access and produce computer records for as long as necessary.

The retention schedule should be distributed throughout the organization to those employees with responsibilities for records creation, maintenance, transfers, media conversions, and destruction. Procedures must be in place for routine and systematic implementation of the records retention schedule, and for documentation of the process.

PROGRAM ADMINISTRATION

A records retention program should be authorized by the chief executive officer, legal counsel, and the tax manager. A company policy statement defines the scope and purpose of the retention program, authorizes implementation of the program, identifies the person responsible for its implementation, and prescribes sanctions for noncompliance with the policy.

But a program that exists only on paper is not good enough. Employees must clearly understand the importance of record-keeping and the guidelines for records retention and destruction. Any destruction outside of a program could appear to be more corrupt than random destruction in the absence of a program, because ill-timed records destruction is subject to misinterpretation. Annual audits or compliance reviews help ensure enforcement if sanctions for noncompliance are provided for in the company policy.

At ForwardThink Corporation, the clout to obtain compliance with the records retention and disposition schedule comes from top management. When an audit of a department reveals problems with implementation of the retention schedule, the offending department is prohibited from purchasing any new equipment, and no facility improvements are authorized for that department. In addition, departmental employees are not eligible for annual company bonuses.

A records retention and disposition coordinator, normally the records and information manager, is ultimately responsible for keeping the program current and for ensuring that microfilming, records transfers, and destruction are done in an orderly manner. In large organizations, this person oversees departmental coordinators in these responsibilities.

The program coordinator develops procedures for smooth operations, for uniform treatment of records, and for periodic reviews of the program. Regular reviews of the retention schedule and disposition practices determine if retention periods are still appropriate, if new regulations or statutes are in force, or if clarification is needed. Changing business functions or legal requirements may affect the way records are maintained, and new records categories may be needed in the retention schedule. The program coordinator also should be familiar enough with the program to be capable of testifying in court if necessary.

Program Documentation

A business may need to demonstrate to a legal or regulatory authority its good-faith efforts to retain and dispose of records in a responsible manner and in accordance with established business practices. Documentation of the records retention and disposition program should be maintained to show systematic development and administration of the program in the normal course of business.

Retention research documentation shows a best effort to find, interpret, and comply with relevant requirements. The process of program development and the procedures to implement the program should be documented, along with appropriate approvals, research, and lists of destroyed records. Changes to the retention schedule and in program procedures should be documented. Records of audits and any follow-up actions or program modifications also should be maintained.

Program documentation should be retained for a reasonable period of time, or as long as is deemed necessary to substantiate the claim that best efforts were made to determine appropriate requirements and that the program was well conceived. Documentation will establish that a program has been implemented in the regular course of business over a period of time.

A client of the ForwardThink Corporation filed a claim against the company and requested documents in pretrial discovery that were only four years old. As it turns out, the desired documents had been destroyed only eight months earlier under the firm's records retention and disposition program. Crying foul, the client asked the court to bring sanctions against ForwardThink because of deliberate destruction of unfavorable records.

ForwardThink Corporation was able to show the court that its records destruction program had been implemented consistently for the last nine years, and that its legal research had found no requirement to retain the documents in question for longer than three years. The judge found in favor of the defendant on this point because of the firm's established program and because there was no evidence that ForwardThink was aware that the client intended to file a claim at the time that the records were destroyed. Because the plaintiff was unable to support his claim without those documents, the charges against the firm were dropped.

Records Organization to Facilitate Program Administration

How well records are indexed and organized will determine how efficiently records disposition is accomplished. A number of benefits will be realized when records are grouped by functional categories with clearly identifiable dates, and when designated record copies are distinguishable from duplicate records.

The final determination of record-keeping requirements is based on the function(s) of a records group. When records are organized in a manner consistent with the retention schedule, it is much easier to apply the retention research findings. A functional grouping of the physical records allows simpler, more efficient filing and retrieval for normal business use, transfers, media conversions, or final destruction. The ability to isolate records having different retention requirements is especially important for computer files, microfilm rolls, microfiche, and larger paper files. The impracticality of applying retention requirements to different records categories that are contained on a unitized computer database or on a single microfilm reel will result in improper administration of the retention schedule.

The ForwardThink Corporation uses a functional and subject listing to organize its records. Very large series of records are further organized by year, including accounts receivables, OSHA reports, policy manuals, job placement files, fixed asset reports, and payroll tax reports.

Corporate standards for computers require that diskettes and tapes contain only similar records groups that have the same retention requirements, and that they be clearly identified to facilitate retrievals and destruction at the appropriate time. Microfilming procedures are similar in that wherever possible and practical, a microfilm reel will not contain records that have different retention requirements.

Because duplicate records may be called into evidence, they must be controlled in much the same way as designated record copies. Any method that clearly distinguishes a designated record copy from a duplicate record will ensure its timely and proper destruction.

Records Disposition

Standardized procedures for records disposition will simplify training and will ensure uniform handling of similar records in all media and in all locations. These instructions may be found in a retention schedule.

The retention schedule may call for a particular records group to be transferred to inactive storage, microfilmed, or disposed of at a certain time. Internal procedures for records transfer should be designed for efficiency and to ensure that any system used to identify the locations of records be updated.

The standard procedures used to convert records from one medium to another should be followed and documented when the schedule calls for media conversion, such as microfilming. These records conversion procedures are based on government, legal, and business record-keeping requirements. The retention schedule should indicate whether or not the original record may be disposed of at the time of conversion or at a later date.

When the retention schedule calls for destruction of a records group, it should also indicate the appropriate disposal method for that records group. Private and proprietary records normally are shredded. If the retention schedule indicates destruction of 50 categories of records at a given time, all 50 groups must be destroyed—not 30 or 40 records groups—in order to prevent any negative inferences. All documents and records groups slated for destruction must be destroyed unless there is a compelling reason not to destroy them, such as foreseeable litigation or government investigation.

Lists of records destroyed according to the retention schedule are maintained to document the retention program's administration. All program documentation may be used to show that records have been routinely destroyed in the ordinary course of business according to consistent, standardized procedures, and that all similar records have been treated alike.

The ForwardThink Corporation wants to make sure that there is complete compliance with its records retention and disposition schedule. Records management staff coordinate the destruction process on an ongoing basis with departmental records coordinators and commercial vendors that are storing company records.

When designated record copies in the possession of a department are slated for destruction, records management staff notify the department to ship those records to ForwardThink's records center. Records center staff confirm that destruction is appropriate, determine the proper destruction method, and document the destruction.

When company records that are maintained by the commercial records center are to be destroyed, records management staff notify the vendor of what records are to be destroyed and the method of destruction. The vendor then provides a certificate of destruction for ForwardThink's retention program documentation.

When a records retention schedule is well developed and regularly updated, there normally would be no need to obtain further approvals for destruction after all the appropriate departments have approved the schedule. However, a business might consider a final review by legal counsel and/or the tax manager prior to destruction in order to discover any important recent changes in the law, or if any litigation or government actions have been initiated and records management has not yet been notified to suspend destruction. If in this final review a decision is made to retain the records longer than the retention schedule indicates, the reason must be justified and documented.

It is irresponsible, and potentially dangerous in a legal sense, to clean house on a whim or when there is a crisis for space—especially when litigation or an investigation is imminent. A retention schedule is a necessary guide to all records disposition, including a one-time record destruction or microfilming project. There should be no haphazard or selective destruction of business records.

The House of Good Intentions has a warehouse full of records from a company that it acquired years earlier. The records have not been used and they appear to be of no value. Because the records have not been organized and indexed for a comparison with its own record retention schedule, random samples are selected to assess their value. A record is made of the categories of files found, including which ones are slated for destruction, and why. The few records found to be of some legal or historical value are microfilmed according to the firm's standard microfilming procedures, the decision-making and filming processes are documented, and the original records are destroyed.

Premature Destruction

Occasionally, a record is lost or destroyed before the expiration of its retention period. Such a mishap occurs primarily through accident or negligence, but occasionally the loss is purposeful. Special procedures may be needed to handle this situation for records in all media.

If a duplicate of the lost record exists, the duplicate would now be considered the record copy. It should be marked as such and stored so that it is subject to the original record's retention requirement. Perhaps the record is available for duplication from an outside source, such as a government agency, customer, or supplier, or the record may be re-created from other existing records.

Legal counsel may deem it necessary to document any premature destruction or loss of a record. This documentation would show that the record did in fact exist at one time, the reason for its loss, and when the loss was discovered. A notarized statement of accidental loss will include a description of the record and the circumstances under which it was lost. One copy of the statement may be stored in place of the original record, and additional copies may be maintained by records management and/or the company's litigation support group. If the original record is needed at a later date for any legal reason, this document would be submitted in place of the original.

Suspension of Destruction

Some records may need to be retained longer than prescribed by the retention schedule. Procedures must be established to suspend normal destruction procedures in the event of foreseeable, pending, or actual litigation or government investigation. This suspended destruction often is referred to as a legal, litigation, or tax hold.

As soon as anyone in the company is aware of such a situation, legal counsel must be notified immediately. Because it can be unclear initially which records will be involved, it is best to stop destruction of all records until legal counsel can determine what records are relevant to the case.

As legal counsel identifies affected records, counsel should notify the records manager of which records are affected, and should grant permission to continue destruction of all other records according to the retention schedule. All employees should be advised of the record destruction suspension for the records affected, and efforts must be made to protect the records from alteration or loss.

11

Integrating Media Choices

Getting the right information to the right user(s) at the right time is a primary objective of records and information management—regardless of the record's form. In today's and tomorrow's business world, information carriers may include paper, microfilm rolls, microfilm cartridges, microfiche, computer disks, computer tapes, computer diskettes, optical disks, audio and video tapes or cassettes, photos, and slides. No single medium is the answer to a company's record-keeping needs. Selection of an information carrier is based on a number of factors, and one record form may be more appropriate than another for certain records. Factors to consider when determining the best media alternative are covered later in this chapter.

Figure 11.1, Business Information Systems, illustrates the many different information systems commonly used in business. Paper, microform, and computer are the primary information systems in use today. Paper and microform records will remain a reality until optical disk—or some other new information carrier—becomes affordable and meets evidentiary and archival requirements. Even if a business proclaims a paperless office, it will not eliminate faxes, photocopiers, or computer printers. Nor will it convert all existing paper or microfilm records to electronic storage, because of the technical problems, prohibitive costs, and legal considerations.

Each of these information systems normally has records migrating to and from other information systems, as shown in the illustration. In the not-too-distant future, it also will be common for the voice, video, and

Figure 11.1
Business Information Systems

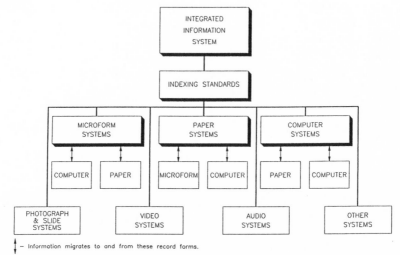

─ Information migrates to and from these record forms.

photograph information systems to have records migrating to and from computer-assisted information systems.

AN INTEGRATED INFORMATION SYSTEM

Every company needs an enterprise-wide information system that is easy to use, easy to manage, and easy to change. End users want their information in a readable form as quickly and as easily as possible, without having first to determine which information system to query when in need of specific information.

Over the years, the management approach to records has focused on form over content. The physical and technical attributes of paper, microfilm, and computer systems have driven their organization and administration. A more appropriate focus on the content of records and information is necessary to meet business and legal record-keeping requirements and information needs. The requirements for speedy and comprehensive record identification, retrieval, processing, and production are more easily and more cost-effectively fulfilled when the form of a record is invisible to the user.

Individual information subsystems will have significant added value when they are integrated into a single information system. Such a system prevents unnecessary duplication and the difficulties in updating information that exist in more than one record form. Many problems may occur when data is inconsistent throughout a company as a result of information systems that are organized and administered independently of each other.

To fully exploit the value of an information subsystem, an integrated information system should be designed before undertaking any new computer or microfilm system. Each subsystem must have a useful indexing system that is compatible with established, uniform indexing standards. Without an adequate indexing system, even a standalone information system will not be a cost-effective information resource. (Imagine searching for a document created by someone else last year, or even last week, and not knowing the document's name or if it is on paper, computer, or microfilm.)

The individual business must determine the best mix of information recording methods to meet its needs. Then, similar to the push for interoperability of multivendor computer systems, each information system will need to coexist and be integrated with other systems. No individual system should compete with or contradict other systems. Information management standards will be necessary to coordinate each information subsystem with all other manual and automated systems. As with the application of computer standards, all records and information systems must be able to interface with other systems for the sharing and distribution of information.

Compatible indexing systems facilitate proper storage, retrieval, and processing of records in all media. Records are identified with distinctive and meaningful titles. Cross-indexing and key word search features enhance the ability to efficiently retrieve specific or similar records in all media.

When information creators and records users talk the same language, common search strategies will improve productivity. Otherwise, differences in data definitions may lead to layering of inconsistent or outdated information and a failure to make relevant associations among records groups and media systems. When systems are fragmented in such a way that data sources cannot be simultaneously updated or searched, unsuspecting users may reference an outdated or incomplete version of information.

An integrated information system has added value when one factors in its support of legal requirements. Administration and control of records procedures from the point of record creation or receipt through final disposition will be more effective. The procedures to create audit trails and systems documentation vary somewhat among the different media, but the task of fulfilling record-keeping requirements is simplified, and the ever-so-important element of consistency will be there.

A tool frequently used to manage an integrated information system is a computerized records management system. Similar to a fixed assets inventory program, the automated technology provides effective management and controls with fewer resources. A computerized records inventory system can go a long way toward improving access to and better management of records in all media from the time of their origination through their eventual disposition.

A bank installed a multiapplication, multidepartmental, image-based optical disk document management system. Among its many applications are accounts payable, mortgage loan insurance files, consumer loans, and credit card management. The system includes a scanner, optical jukebox, laser printer, controller, magnetic storage, and remote display terminals. A uniform indexing system allows a single search path for all documents, regardless of their storage medium—optical disk, microfilm, or paper. The work of seven file clerks is now done by one employee, turnaround time for system users has decreased, and customer service has improved.

MEDIA DECISIONS

Foresight is needed to determine the best method to meet present and future requirements of end users, the government, rules of evidence, preservation and cost-effectiveness. Strategic goals for information management should support long-range decisions regarding technology, equipment, facilities, and the wise allocation of resources. A business must consider the potential growth of its information system(s), growth of specific records classes, and any potential interfaces with other technologies or systems.

When designing any information system, a business must look at information integrity, record use, security, retention, and potential legal considerations. Various information technologies and alternative media are evaluated for their adaptability to meet these requirements.

- What are the needs of primary and secondary users for retrieval speed, duplication, processing and updating?

- What information storage devices are available (paper, diskettes, microforms, optical disks, etc.), and what are their capacities for information storage?

- How long must the records be retained, how quickly will they grow in volume, and what are the constraints on space to store each medium and any necessary equipment to process the information?
- What are the technical, security, system documentation, or other requirements associated with each information carrier and records group?
- What are the costs associated with each information carrier?

Legal Status

A number of legal requirements may affect media selection and administration. A contract may have record media requirements, and rules of evidence may specify the conditions under which a duplicate, microform, or computer record is allowed.

Most requirements today that directly impact media choice are for microfilm records, but efforts are underway to update regulations and statutes on information to reflect the latest information technologies. Federal agencies that have microfilm procedural and technical requirements are:

- Department of Agriculture
- Department of Energy
- Energy Regulatory Commission
- Environmental Protection Agency
- Federal Communications Commission
- Federal Deposit Insurance Corporation
- Federal Drug Administration
- Internal Revenue Service
- Department of Justice
- Department of Labor
- Nuclear Regulatory Commission
- Securities and Exchange Commission
- Department of Transportation

In the event that any restrictions exist regarding destruction of the original record, it may not be cost-effective for a business to plan a conversion of records to microform or computer. There are occasions when the original must be maintained and made available for inspection by an agency or court. In other situations, the original may be filmed and then destroyed only after a designated number of years. Contractual obligations may prohibit destruction of original records, as when records are maintained in a fiduciary or custodial capacity. And federal contractors normally may not destroy the original unless certain conditions are met.

When there is no legal requirement for the form of a record, a business is free to choose whatever media will meet the record's retention and information security requirements, and its own needs. Any stipulated records retention or information security requirements may help determine the appropriate media choice. They also may detail procedures to follow in the event of record damage or loss.

The trustworthiness of a record—regardless of its medium—may be questioned. Almost all information statutes were written when records were maintained exclusively on paper. Such statutes and rules of evidence will need to be updated to include computer, optical disk, voice messaging, electronic mail, video, and so on. Until then, audit trails and documentation on the creation, processing, and production of paper, microform, data processing, and imaging system records may be necessary. When a record reproduction program is challenged, the business may need to prove that the filming or duplication was done in the normal course of business or that the record is an accurate reproduction of the original.

As the traditional information carrier, paper is challenged the least often regarding its authenticity. An original paper record is most valuable when the record's authenticity is questioned or when it is the only means to provide a legible duplicate record. Occasionally it is preferable to maintain an original in order to preserve its physical characteristics, such as paper texture, age, color, or size.

Microforms generally are admissible as original records, though the reproduction process or the authenticity of the original may be questioned. Procedural and documentation requirements for microform records may include:

- statement of subject matter on the film
- indexing and arrangement of the information
- name of the department or person authorizing the filming process
- camera operator name and date
- certificate of authenticity
- reproduction procedures, timetable and film odometer readings

- quality inspections of records
- film splicing procedures

The trustworthiness of computer records is more likely to come under scrutiny because these records are more easily altered without a trace. Computer records requirements can be quite cumbersome when they call for extensive system documentation that may not already exist in a company's business practices. Documentation that may be needed to dismiss any trustworthiness challenge includes:

- records creation or conversion procedures
- verification of data validity
- software and operating systems documentation
- data processing procedures
- computer operations log
- audit trail from data entry to production of a visible record
- database modifications
- production of visible records in the ordinary course of business

As more government agencies allow electronic records under certain conditions, maintenance of additional system documentation may be required, as follows:

- system manuals
- file and document listings
- source and object codes
- make and model numbers of tape and disk devices
- interface requirements

Record Permanence and Durability

A record's retention requirement and its anticipated use will determine what permanence and durability characteristics will be necessary in the information carrier and any system used to process the information. If a record has a relatively short retention period, it is more cost-effective to place that record on a less costly medium. For example, paper trash that is microfilmed or scanned onto an optical disk becomes a very expensive and nonbiodegradable trash. The longer the retention requirement for a record, the more important are the permanence and durability characteristics of its selected information carrier and any information processing equipment.

A business may need to take steps to prevent technical obsolescence and degradation of its information carriers and processors. Some information carriers are self-destructive, and all information carriers and information processors are vulnerable to aging, obsolescence, poor environmental conditions, and misuse. Acidic paper, poor duplication techniques and processing, and computer tapes and diskettes are examples of self-destructive information carriers. Microforms are a safe information carrier that may last for an extended number of years under good conditions. The physical properties of audio recordings are such that they last only a few years, so the information must be transcribed to some other more dependable medium.

Many businesses today install new computer systems every few years. Those records may be subject to an IRS or other government investigation for ten or more years. In such a situation, the older data should be converted to the new system, or the old system should be maintained and the records made available for as long as the information may be needed by the government or by the business.

Computer diskettes, hard disks, and computer tapes generally last less than ten years, but they may be copied and recopied as needed. Though time has not yet proven optical disk to be an archival medium, manufacturers are quoting lifetimes of ten to one hundred years, depending on the quality of the disk. From all indications today, optical disk is the only computer record that may be considered archival, assuming that the hardware and software required will be available and functioning when the records will be needed.

Hardware and software may become obsolete or dysfunctional in even shorter periods of time. Information may become stranded on tapes from primitive or discarded systems. Government data from 20 years ago has decomposed to the point where it will fall apart if run through any surviving equipment from that era. A company may need new software to decipher the old programs and reorganize the data before a new system is able to analyze and process the information. Occasionally, system documentation does not exist or media are not properly labeled, rendering the information useless.

Security

Individual records groups may have different security requirements. Federal contractors in the possession of classified information must comply with federal guidelines for the equipment and facilities that house such information. Certain government agencies may have other information security requirements. A company also will want to safeguard certain records to preserve legal rights and to meet its own needs.

Records and information in all media may need to be protected from loss, damage, alteration, or unauthorized access. Some media are more secure than others for protection of records from specific threats, and security measures will vary from one medium to another. Sight-readable records will require equipment and facility modifications to prevent unauthorized access, damage, or loss. Machine-readable records may require security measures unique to the system to prevent unauthorized access or accidental destruction.

Organization and Use

Understanding the function(s) of a record and how it will be used help determine what information carrier is most useful and how best to organize it.

- Who will use the information and how often will it be used?
- Will there be any restrictions on access to the record?
- How long will the information be needed by users?
- Will user needs change over time?
- What equipment will be required to access, process, and produce records?

Access efficiencies are lowest for large volumes of paper records. An overriding need for simultaneous and instantaneous access by a number of users typically is the justification for a computer records system. Microforms may not be as costly as computer records, given their low duplication and distribution costs, but access is not as fast as with computer records.

Indexing and organization of various media will vary somewhat within standard guidelines. With a good indexing system, computer records can be retrieved and filed more quickly and more accurately than microform or paper records. The uniform sizes and fixed-file continuity character-istics of microforms provide for more convenient and accurate filing than is the case with that of paper records. Records groups that have different retention requirements should be organized on separate tapes, diskettes, film reels, microfiche, or file folders, to avoid compromising the integrity of a records destruction program.

Cost Considerations

Cost is a significant factor in the selection of a record form. Among the costs to consider are usage, storage, security, and any process necessary to convert records from one medium to another. Paper records are costly to store and retrieve in terms of space, equipment, and human resources. Duplication and distribution of microforms are less costly than distribution of large volumes of paper. Computer and microform records will require hardware or equipment to create, read, process and produce the records.

The costs to store microforms are less than those for paper, in spite of the expense for microform readers and reader-printers.

- As little as 5 percent of the space and equipment required for paper records is required for those same records in microform.
- A single 100-foot roll of film, or ten microfiche, are the equivalent of approximately 2,600 feet of continuous computer printout.
- An estimated 5,000 pages of documents may be contained on only 25 double-density diskettes, which may be filed in the same space as required for only 200 paper documents.
- A single 12-inch optical disk holds approximately 500,000 pages of text or 100,000 images. The contents of 13 four-drawer cabinets will fit on one optical disk that holds 140,000 documents.

Though microform and computer records require less storage expense, other cost considerations could rule them out as a media choice. Computer system installation costs may be prohibitive. (Optical disk systems today cost ten times more than a microform system.) It may be difficult to justify conversion of records to another form when the costs to store the original record are lower than the costs to convert and store the records in the new form. Paper conversion costs include preparation of the paper record, filming or scanning, film processing, quality control, indexing, and the subsequent storage, handling, use, and equipment necessary to read and produce the records. These costs increase when documents are folded, images are on both sides of a document, images are faded, or there are variations in the size, color, or weight of the papers.

INFORMATION CARRIERS

The number of information carriers has grown over the years, along with the number of their records applications. The next section describes the three primary information carriers used in business today.

Paper

Paper is an information carrier that business will be managing well into the twenty-first century, and beyond. Even companies that can afford optical disk today will not convert all of their paper records that are piled up in storage areas.

Paper is not always as long-lasting a medium as one hopes. It may suffer damage or loss from physical deterioration due to biological, chemical, or mechanical causes. Natural disasters and planned or inadvertent actions by people also may affect the continued existence of paper records.

The acid content in paper weakens and breaks the paper's fibers, causing the paper to yellow and become brittle. Today's newspaper is yellow next week, and brittle enough to break into pieces in a few years. Well into the nineteenth century, most paper was manufactured using cotton or linen rags. Demand eventually exceeded supply, forcing paper makers to turn to wood pulp, bleaching, sizing, and chemical processes that create a high acid content in the paper. Acids in paper originate from the chemicals used in the manufacturing process, printing inks and dyes, human hands, air pollutants, and other materials with which paper comes in contact.

The method used to record information on paper also may contribute to permanence and durability problems. Certain inks can contaminate an otherwise permanent paper. The use of dark blue and black inks is preferred for signatures because they resist fading, and durability of carbonless paper copies may be an issue. Hard ballpoint pens leave a physical impression in the paper that may be useful in the event that the ink fades. Certain typewriter ribbons are susceptible to letters lifting off of the paper, thus obliterating the information.

The role of the facsimile record continues to grow, and it will expand as plain paper machines continue to fall in price. According to one industry analyst, more than 12 billion pages of documents were sent by fax machine in 1990. But thermal fax paper is not a satisfactory information carrier: it turns brown and the print fades with age or exposure to sunlight and heat. It also is difficult to write notations on a thermal paper document.

Microform

Microform is a generic name used to describe any of the various forms in which the use of microphotography reproduces a record. A microform may be a microfilm, a microfiche, or an aperture card. The poor quality of the original record or legal considerations may not always make filming practical or feasible. The conditions under which microforms are most suitable are:

- filing and space problems exist
- information integrity must be preserved
- the records are to be retained for seven or more years
- the same records are needed in separate locations
- security copies of vital, optical disk, or other records are necessary

The type of microform selected will depend on the anticipated uses of the records and how frequently the records will be updated. If information security and file integrity are more important than the ability to update the information, unitized film formats are recommended, such as microfilm rolls and microfiche. Roll film is serialized on open reels, cartridges, or cassettes, and may be updated only by splicing. Recent developments in microfiche allow it to be updated, and some microfiche is now erasable. However, these new features for altering film records may have a negative impact on the trustworthiness of a record.

Microfilm jackets containing film strips are easily updated and, like microfiche, permit direct access to the desired image without having to advance through a roll of film. Computer assisted retrieval (CAR) systems can film documents in random order, indexing and coding them as the batch of records is filmed, and then enter the indexing information into a computer system. Functioning as a computer database manager, a CAR system provides for efficient updating and cross-referencing of records by directing the user to a designated frame for the record desired.

Records may be filmed directly from paper records through source document micrographics, or microforms may be created directly from electronic records. Computer output microfilm (COM) is created by the transfer of data directly from a computer to microfilm without the necessity to create paper. Production costs are greatly reduced when paper record creation is eliminated.

The permanence of a microform is governed by the quality of the film and processing, the storage conditions, and its usage. Conformance with microfilm industry standards will reduce the concerns about obsolescence and compatibility of associated equipment that presently exist with electronic records. Silver halide film supports permanent or archival standards of quality. Diazo film has an inherent dye fade, but it is less expensive and more suitable for temporary use. Any existing nitrate-based film records must be copied to another film and disposed of properly, as it may spontaneously combust at temperatures of 106 degrees Fahrenheit or higher, giving off toxic gases.

Computer Media

The use of computers in business first started with data processing applications, and is now moving into database, text, and image management. There are hybrid systems of electronic or digital and photographic or microform information systems. The more advanced systems can scan, microfilm, digitize, read, print, transfer to optical disk, or transmit records via facsimile or local area network (LAN.) Not too far in the future are voice and video management systems with business applications.

As storage and retrieval systems, computer information systems reduce storage requirements, protect records from loss, reduce search times, provide immediate access by multiple users to the same record, and distribute information faster to end users. With an adequate indexing system, filing and retrieval costs are low and there are few "lost" files. Certain system procedures may protect data from alteration or loss caused by users.

Electronic or document imaging systems are available in sizes from a desktop model to a mainframe computer that accesses a jukebox of optical disks. Computer-generated, paper, or microform images are stored on high-capacity optical disks. Imaging systems are cost-effective for large-volume, high-use records that do not need updating. Magneto-optical disks and other erasable disks allow data changes, thus complicating issues related to rules of evidence. System documentation and documentation of the procedures followed for records conversion and production may prove useful for purposes of showing trustworthiness of the records. When permanence and legal issues are settled, and prices become more affordable, electronic imaging will be hard to beat for records storage economies.

In the rush to install systems in hopes of solving office productivity problems, many businesses have not thoroughly thought out the impact of computer technologies on record-keeping requirements. A business loses control of its records on personal computer systems scattered throughout the facility without standards in place. Many of the desktop and mainframe systems are not designed to work with other computer, paper-based, or microform information systems. Nor are many systems designed to comply with the record-keeping requirements of the records contained on the system. Among the concerns and unanswered questions about computer information systems are:

- Who will use the information, and how will they find it?

- How long must the records be retained, and is the system capable of maintaining and processing them for that long?

- Will parts, service, and system support be available for as long as may be necessary?

- If there is a possibility the information will be needed by the government or a court, will it hold up as evidence?

- What controls will be necessary to ensure that information is systematically and accurately collected, generated, maintained, produced, distributed, and destroyed?

- Is there adequate security to protect information from damage, loss, or unauthorized access?

- Is the system compatible with other information systems—including computer, paper, and microform?

STORAGE CONDITIONS AND HANDLING REQUIREMENTS

Storage conditions and how records are handled will affect access capabilities and the permanence and durability of a record medium. The appropriate storage and handling conditions and practices must exist to help preserve records and make them accessible for the necessary time period. Periodic inspections to check the condition of each medium for deterioration or damage from storage conditions or handling may be necessary.

Environment

Storage conditions that are the enemy of information carriers are high temperatures, humidity extremes, ultraviolet light radiation, atmospheric pollutants, and various biological entities. Damage to media from adverse environmental conditions generally is not reversible.

Temperature and humidity levels that are consistent with energy conservation and worker comfort guidelines are generally acceptable for records. The lower the temperature, the better. High humidity promotes mold and bacteria growth and accelerates deterioration caused by acids in materials. Mold degrades paper cellulose fibers and will stain and discolor records. If humidity is too low, materials tend to become brittle. High temperatures and humidity also favor the propagation of pests that eat paper, glue, photos, and other materials.

Wide fluctuations in heat and moisture will stress materials as they expand and contract. A stabilized temperature of between 55 and 65 degrees Fahrenheit and a relative humidity of 40 percent to 50 percent are close to ideal for a multimedia storage facility. Fluctuations of more than 10 degrees or 15 percent relative humidity from hour to hour, day to day, or season to season should be avoided.

The heat given off by light sources is relatively insignificant when compared to the damage that may be caused by the ultraviolet radiation from natural sunlight and fluorescent light. Records should be stored away from direct sunlight, or the windows should be covered. Incandescent lighting should be used whenever possible because it emits no harmful radiation, or fluorescent lighting tubes may be fitted with ultraviolet radiation filter sleeves.

A number of air pollutants and destructive gases emitted from building materials, equipment, and a growing number of records themselves need to be controlled. Any dust or grime in the presence of moisture can act as a corrosive poultice. Gaseous and other particulate pollutants in the air may soil paper, contribute to acidic deterioration of paper or microfilm, or obliterate data contained on microform or computer media. Air pollutants also may cause damage to equipment, which could then damage the information medium.

Fire, heat, and water also take their toll on paper, microforms, computer records, magnetic tapes, photographs, and other media. A business may want to take any steps necessary to prevent or minimize threats from a number of disasters and to produce backup records for storage elsewhere in the event of records loss. Because salvage procedures for different media may vary, any disaster plan should address these concerns.

Preservation and Handling

Records preservation encompasses the efforts to retard or control deterioration or to prevent the loss of records. The extent of preservation efforts for different records will depend on the value(s) of the records and how long they must be maintained.

The equipment, hardware, and software required to read, process, produce, and store information in various media must be well maintained and functioning properly to prevent damage or loss of information. Harmful acids, oils, and dirt easily migrate from media containers or hands to records, so consideration of plastic or acid-free folders or boxes may be appropriate to house certain records, and excessive records handling should be avoided. Electronic and magnetic media should be kept away from magnetic or static sources.

12

Organization and Staffing for the Records Function

The visible commitment of senior officials is essential for any organization-wide records and information management program. As the executives and their lawyers buy into the records management concept and its benefits, this commitment must flow down from top management through the operating managers to all employees. Only when the support of operations personnel exists can there be program compliance. The decision-makers throughout a business must understand how a records and information management program contributes to the success and livelihood of the business as a whole, as well as to their specific business activities, and that the function is not an option.

A company policy on records and information assets, and the means to enforce that policy, must be endorsed by the company's executives. The objectives of information retrieval and compliance with government and judicial record-keeping requirements should be top priorities in the policy. Beyond that should be concerns about protecting records in order to continue doing business and to protect the business from unnecessary liabilities.

Senior management further demonstrates their support by the allocation of necessary resources—equipment and staffing—to meet planned objectives, and by transferring authority to the right people. As a cost of doing business, the records management expense is an investment in several long-term benefits:

• improved efficiencies

- reduced storage and handling costs
- controls to more effectively manage the business and to properly manage and protect company information assets

ORGANIZATIONAL STRUCTURE

Someone, regardless of title, must have overall responsibility for records and information management and for keeping up on relevant regulations, issues, and trends. The corporate secretary is ultimately responsible for records in corporations. Executive management empowers its directors and managers with responsibilities and the appropriate authority to implement company policy. This responsibility normally is assigned to a single employee and department. The size of a business, how it is structured, the nature of its records and information systems, and the records program objectives help determine the best place in the organization for this important business function.

In most organizations, records management is a staff or support function, not a line function. Although records management does not always have its own place on a company's organization chart, its functions do exist under various managers' areas of responsibilities. Whether one person or several share the records function, every employee shares the benefits and the responsibilities.

What department is ultimately responsible for records management will vary from one company to another. In a minority of organizations, records management is left to the finance department. The justification typically is that the finance department holds the bulk of the company's records. However, such an approach loses sight of the fact that other important records exist and that records management involves a wide range of issues beyond departmental records and information needs.

In light of the unique interrelationship of business law and records management, there are advocates of placing the records management function directly under the law department or assigning one attorney the responsibility and accountability for records management. At the very least, a strong and clearly defined liaison between legal and records management is necessary to effectively implement policies and procedures that fulfill government, legal, and fiduciary responsibilities.

A growing number of organizations are placing records management with the MIS department. This is a step in the right direction, as it integrates paper and computer records.

Most companies traditionally place records management with administrative services, along with word processing, micrographics, reprographics, telecommunications, and the mail room. These activities are an organization's support systems, which cross departmental lines to provide necessary services throughout the business. If the records and information management function does not have its own place on the organization chart, placing it with administration would probably be preferable, as long as the program is comprehensive and has the appropriate support and enforcement from senior management.

Ideally, the records management function originates with the start-up of a company. A new organization presents the unique opportunity to start off on the right foot and avoid having to resolve records problems later after they have developed. A program's flexibility to support business growth and change is especially important in this situation.

Small businesses are less likely to hire a records manager or specialist because the economies of scale do not exist to justify dedicated support staff. Records management tasks then tend to be lumped with other tasks and assigned to various job positions. One person, usually the office manager, must learn to handle many of the aspects of records management. Typically, that employee is not knowledgeable enough to do the job well for every aspect of a program. Usually the records activities fall to the bottom of the list of priorities as other duties become more pressing.

The TechTrack firm cannot justify the cost of a new job position for a records manager. Instead, the director of administrative services is responsible for the records management program. The office manager is the liaison between this director and the records coordinators in every department and branch location. The director of administrative services has hired a records management consultant to establish a basic framework for policies and practices that meet the company's needs. The director has also contracted with the company's outside legal counsel to establish a records retention schedule. A task force has put together a vital records schedule and a disaster plan. Another ongoing committee works on issues related to media selection and various information systems that are in the planning stages. A commercial records center stores and manages inactive records and backup computer tapes.

Larger businesses can afford a records staff, including:

- a records and information manager, or chief information officer
- records analysts
- file clerks
- records center personnel
- micrographics technicians
- litigation support specialists
- proprietary information coordinator
- vital records coordinator
- other support staff

In large organizations, the records manager and support staff usually work out of the headquarters office, and are responsible for the development of standard policies and practices that support all office sites.

The ForwardThink Corporation has a records manager located at its headquarters office. This manager develops standard practices that simplify records management activities throughout the company. Among these standards are indexing and filing system guidelines to reduce training costs and to facilitate records retrieval and transfer.

To maintain control over records and to relieve field offices of certain record-keeping burdens and expenses, designated records categories are the responsibility of the headquarters departments or records staff. These records include employee files, financial records, and original contracts and agreements. When a branch office needs information contained in these files, it relies on a duplicate copy or requests a copy from headquarters.

The records manager works with the MIS department to establish corporate-wide indexing and retention standards for desktop and mainframe computer records. The manager also works with the director of corporate security to establish information security policies and practices. The law department maintains a current records retention schedule that is administered by the records manager. The records manager supervises the off-site microfilming of all corporate records.

Coordinating Relationships

Because records management involves so many diverse objectives and activities, it may very well be appropriate to assign specific activities to different positions. The key to program success then becomes having a single point to coordinate the pieces that constitute a whole program.

A network of interdepartmental relationships is required for close cooperation in the development of an effective information resource management policy and its supporting standards and practices. The benefits of working with other departments may be realized in the cosponsorship of training programs, better employee communications, and development of policies, procedures, and standards that are acceptable to everyone involved. Such relationships also avoid conflicting procedures among the departments and avoid reinventing the wheel.

Functional areas or departments most critical to the development and support of a records and information management program include:

- records and information users
- top management
- legal
- internal audit staff
- MIS/data processing
- administration
- security
- risk management
- facility planning
- purchasing
- corporate archives

More specifically, MIS staff and lawyers could benefit, and make better contributions to the business, by learning a little about records management, just as the records manager needs to develop some expertise in the areas of law and computer information systems. Records, MIS, and legal staff need to talk with each other about:

- government and legal record-keeping requirements
- information security
- identification and protection of vital records

- a corporate disaster plan
- records retention
- the integration of information systems

The records manager needs to sit down with managers from these various functional areas to clarify responsibilities and to determine the issues and activities on which to more effectively focus the scarce resources of people and dollars. These relationships not only provide for a more effective program, they also establish the support base for the program that is so badly needed in business today. The records manager must build a coalition that understands the stakes involved in redefining their purposes, methods, and success, and that has a stronger impact on records users and their information systems.

The larger the organization, the more necessary is a records and information advisory group. Responsibilities for certain company-wide issues are spread out over a committee of subject experts. Committee members are the organization's decision-makers who:

- provide technical expertise and advice
- develop corporate-wide procedures and standards
- approve retention and vital records schedules
- advise on media selection and information security

As the committee chairperson, the records manager coordinates the various interrelated activities scattered throughout the organization.

PROGRAM ELEMENTS

A comprehensive records and information management program integrates a number of elements, not all of which typically wind up as a records manager's direct responsibilities. However, each program element must be coordinated by the records management function and integrated to achieve a value greater than the sum of its parts. When one or more components breaks down, a company may be vulnerable to information risks in a way similar to those experienced when there is no records management program at all.

There is truly no right way to manage records and information—only a smart way that fits the individual organization. The extent and formality of program development and implementation will vary from one business to another. Elements of a comprehensive records and information management program may include the following:

- program objectives
- standards
- multimedia management and integration
- indexing and filing systems
- records centers
- records retention and disposition
- vital records protection
- information security
- archives
- library services
- program administration

Each of these program elements is interrelated with others in the overall effort to provide a records and information program that is supportive of business goals. One must recognize that trade-offs among the various program elements may be necessary. For example, the organization that requires tight information security usually must give up a degree of records access, or a business that requires paper records to support a heavy litigation load will give up any space savings that may be achieved through electronic records storage.

Program Objectives

Program objectives provide for consistent identification, continued existence, and efficient retrievability of valuable and useful records and information. Objectives help focus efforts and promote clear communications with records users. They also must change throughout program development, and as business needs and legal considerations change.

Standards

Standards improve controls and efficiencies, and they help prepare the way for any computer system. Standards reduce the high costs of training and the costs resulting from inconsistencies in records handling. They facilitate certain corporate changes by streamlining decision-making and implementation with minimal disruption of operations. The records manager identifies areas where standards may improve cost-effectiveness, improve productivity, and ensure compliance with record-keeping requirements. Typical records management areas for standards include:

- copy management
- equipment, supplies, and office technologies
- filing systems
- forms design and management
- indexing systems
- media selection
- procedures
- records security and retention practices
- technical terms

Media Management and Integration

Selection of the form for the recording and preservation of information is based on business, legal, and retention requirements. A number of legal requirements may affect both media selection and how the record is created and maintained. The permanence and durability characteristics of a medium, and any system used to process the information, also help determine the most appropriate medium for record creation and maintenance. (See Chapter 11, "Integrating Media Choices," for more information on media decisions.)

The various information media used by a business must be integrated into a uniform information resource that meets users' requirements for access, processing, and document production. Bridges may be necessary to connect any existing islands of information systems. The records manager will need to be involved in the planning processes for any new information systems, such as optical disk, COM, CAR, text management, or microfilm.

Indexing and Filing Systems

Indexing and filing standards are methods of organizing records. The form(s) of records and the method(s) selected to organize them help determine the choice of supplies and equipment. From there, facility design applications are called upon for working with the equipment, access, security, and environmental conditions required for the records.

A standard indexing system superimposed on all company records and information is a must for improved productivity, central filing systems, and the integration of media systems. Though much forethought and effort must go into development of a useful indexing system, it will pay off later in long-term benefits.

Filing systems for active records may be centralized, decentralized, or a form of controlled decentralized systems. In a decentralized system, the user has the high-use records located close by and typically has complete control over them. This situation tends to cause unnecessary duplication throughout the company and, in the absence of indexing standards, the information usually is not accessible by others in the company. Controls over security and records retention may be nonexistent, resulting in unnecessary costs and exposure to liabilities. Records from incompatible filing systems are eventually dumped on a records center, where they remain unretrievable without the additional expense to properly organize and index them.

Centralized filing systems provide cost savings, improved access by multiple users, and better control over records conversions, transfers, and destruction. However, centralized filing systems do not meet user needs for immediate access unless they are electronic filing systems that are networked to individual work stations.

The controlled decentralized files concept is an ideal compromise between immediate access by departmental users and the overall business need for standards and controls. Departments maintain their own files, but all departmental files and records center files are organized by uniform indexing methods and are maintained according to records management standards.

Records Centers

The primary purpose of a records center is to reduce records storage costs. Many centers also are used to provide special security for certain records. A records retention schedule establishes guidelines for when inactive records may be transferred to the less expensive space, and a vital records schedule identifies valuable records to be protected in an off-site facility.

Records centers may be on site or off site. An on-site records center normally stores records that are not actively used in a department but that are still needed occasionally by a number of users throughout the company. Off-site records centers normally store inactive records, as well as vital records in need of special protection.

Retention and Disposition

A records retention schedule determines what records are to be created and maintained, in what form(s), and when they are to be transferred to a records center, converted to another medium, or destroyed. Responsibility for recycling may be added to the records destruction responsibilities. The retention schedule is based on legal requirements and business needs. Procedures must be in place to suspend records destruction in the event of a litigation, tax, or government investigation hold.

Vital Records Protection

A vital records schedule identifies records essential to continuation of business in the event of a disaster, and how they are to be protected. A disaster prevention and recovery program establishes procedures to protect these records, minimize records damage or loss, and resume business as quickly as possible.

Information Security

Safeguarding valuable and sensitive information contributes to a company's overall competitive advantage and protection. There are a number of potential threats to the security of records and information that must be assessed and responded to accordingly. Corporate policies and procedures will contribute to the proper protection of a company's records and information.

Archives

Whether one year old or one hundred years old, every business has records to be retained for long periods of time. Larger and older businesses tend to have formally organized archives for their historical and other important records with extensive retention periods. A business still in its youth will want to review today's business records that could be tomorrow's valuable corporate history. In the absence of a corporate archivist, the records manager is the most likely individual to assume archival responsibilities.

The archives identify, collect, and index historical documents for reference to the extent that executive management has determined the relative value of corporate history. Preservation of archival records requires expertise and appropriate facilities, equipment, and supplies.

Library Services

Library resources and services may support business activities such as staff development, research and development, and marketing. Commercial information databases, subscriptions, training materials, and technical publications can be very expensive and should be managed for optimum return on the investment by centralization of these resources to make them available to all departments and employees.

Not every business needs a corporate library or is in a position to set up a library. Library services normally are administered by the primary-user department or by administrative services. Occasionally, a records manager oversees a library. At the very least, the records manager's input may help promote the management of all information resources as a single support system that enhances access to all information throughout the company.

PROGRAM ADMINISTRATION

A records manager normally is responsible for the systematic development and integration of the records and information management program elements, and for the program's ongoing administration. A comprehensive records and information management program, as described earlier in this chapter, is developed over a period of time. How a program is developed over time will differ from one business to another, based on the financial and human resources committed to the effort. A critical success factor for any approach to program development is the expertise available to coordinate all program activities toward providing a single information resource that meets the company's needs of today and tomorrow.

Program Documentation

Documentation related to the records and information management program is useful in program management, training, and communications activities. Program documentation also is necessary for compliance with government record-keeping requirements. The requirement to maintain company policies and procedures applies to records program documentation. Documentation may be required related to selection and administration of various media—specifically microform and computer. Program documentation also may be needed to satisfy concerns about the trustworthiness of records and any challenges to the nonexistence of certain records.

Records and information management program documentation may be created and maintained on the following topics:

- computer systems
- information security practices
- microphotography practices
- policies and procedures
- program changes
- program evaluations and audits
- retention and destruction

The Records and Information Manager

Essentially, the records and information manager is a consultant and advisor to the business, and a provider of controls and support services that are essential to successful business operations. The manager is responsible for:

- program development and administration
- auditing program compliance
- facilities management
- staff management
- budgeting
- customer service
- a host of other duties

There are records managers today who are well educated and well trained in the disciplines of records management, business administration, library administration, and other fields. Most records managers participate in professional organizations, records management certification programs, and continuing education. A number of organizations focus on information security, document preservation, facilities management, and other areas of interest to a records manager. Professional associations of interest include ARMA International, AIIM, the Institute of Certified Records Managers, the National Association of Government Records Administrators, and the Society of American Archivists.

Records management has become ever more complex and demanding over the years. New office technologies, records preservation challenges, legal considerations, and other concerns, are making the job ever more complicated. As records problems grow in volume and complexity, the records manager needs a wide range of management skills and a high level of technical expertise in a number of areas.

There is a shortage today of records managers who are qualified to manage a comprehensive records and information program. The ideal records manager is familiar with current records and information management technologies and developing trends, changing business information needs, and relevant legal issues. This individual must thoroughly understand records and information management principles and program administration for a number of information media. An effective manager is capable of a broad focus to satisfy the information needs throughout an organization.

General management skills include budgeting, cost analysis, staff management, facilities planning, and purchasing. Given that records management traditionally is not as well supported as it should be, excellent communications and training skills are essential to promote unpopular and poorly understood activities. The records manager must be willing to be proactive in the development of supportive and coordinating relationships throughout the organization.

Staff Management

Many records activities are clerical tasks, but on-the-job training often is required for even these simple tasks. Keeping good clerical staff may be a problem because of the low salaries, monotonous work, and little opportunity for advancement. To attract and keep good employees, and to reduce the high costs of turnover, the records manager may consider redesign of jobs, upgrade of job titles and salaries, and job enrichment.

As the start-up of any new program requires more time, effort, and resources than are required to maintain a program, the records manager may turn to innovative staffing alternatives to accomplish major projects or the start-up of a program. Supplementary human resources may be found both within and outside the company.

Departmental records coordinators in larger organizations occasionally may be able to take on more than their daily records activities. If another department is experiencing a slack period, temporary reassignment of employees from that department could benefit the employee through new experiences and will improve utilization of available human resources. The records manager also may be able to draw on expertise from other departments to produce publications, procedures, or training programs. Retired employees and employees on disability are an excellent source of temporary help that already knows the company. Depending on the tasks and the disability, employees on disability could be productive until they are able to resume their normal duties.

Temporary personnel agencies are outside sources of assistance for major projects and conversions. A community service program may be developed to hire high school students or disabled individuals for specific assignments. Vendors and suppliers may be knowledgeable sources for technical expertise.

Certain records activities may be contracted out to a vendor on a temporary or long-term basis. Commercial records centers store inactive records and provide security for computer data and vital records. The number of firms dedicated to providing litigation support services is growing. Micrographics service bureaus manage microfilming projects, and computer service bureaus collect, maintain, and process electronic information for their clients. Additional outside sources include training consultants, forms management services, archival document conservation centers, and information research services.

A records management consultant may be hired to identify the most critical records management issues and propose alternatives for their resolution. A consultant can be most helpful in setting up the basic framework of a program for ongoing administration by existing records staff. Typical consultant contributions are:

- employee communications and training
- indexing and filing systems development
- policy and program documentation
- records management computer system implementation
- records media conversions
- records or micrographics center design
- retention research

Training and Employee Communications

Every permanent and temporary employee needs a certain degree of records and information management training. As with human resources or accounting policies and practices, all employees may be affected by or may be responsible for compliance with records management policies and practices. Training and communications should begin with the first day of employment and be ongoing throughout employment.

Employee training and communications activities may be developed to target the different records user groups, management levels, and departments. All employees need an understanding of the big picture beyond their specific job functions, department, or the records center. Periodic audits of employee records management skills and knowledge will identify areas for improvement and innovation in training activities.

An overview for all new employees could cover legal requirements, information security, and efficiencies and cost-savings achievable from proper record-keeping practices. Certain employee groups will need somewhat more extensive training to raise levels of awareness regarding media choices, active and inactive records filing systems, and legal issues. Departmental records coordinators, MIS staff, office employees, and other work groups will need more detailed procedural training.

Training and communications may be as simple as a group meeting with handouts and print or electronic news bulletins. Or they may be as elaborate as a multimedia format or video teleconferencing. Training materials may include:

- a general corporate records and information management manual
- more specific departmental manuals
- a records computer system manual and computer user aid
- a handbook to cover indexing standards, file purge procedures, etc., for electronic and other nonprint records

Purchasing and Facilities Management

The records manager normally is responsible for the management of records facilities and for the purchase of goods and services. Facility management begins with the determination of space requirements based on data from a records inventory, any records management computer system, and user needs. The volume of records, their media types, and retention requirements determine how much and what kind of space will be needed.

Purchasing activities include working within the company's procurement policies and practices to develop standards and specifications for the purchase of equipment, supplies, and services. The objective of records management purchasing activities is to buy the most affordable product or service that meets records user needs and the requirements for permanence and durability of records.

Computer System

Installation of a records management computer system improves controls and provides more efficient management of records and information. Administration of the records management program is simplified when a system provides records retention and vital records schedule information and instructions. A system also provides audit trails of records activities, program documentation, and management reports.

A computer system that is media-transparent and based on a sound manual system helps identify unnecessary duplication and inefficient layering of information. An effective manual system should be set up in anticipation of a computerized system, or the computer system should be designed to correct problems in the manual system. Regardless, any dysfunctional process should not be automated.

A wide range of packages and applications is available to meet the needs of different organizations. In the most simplistic form, a computer records management system is an inventory of records and their locations. A typical program tracks records throughout their entire life cycle and contains the final retention periods for records. Programs also are available to organize and assess results of legal research on record-keeping requirements. The most advanced systems will send a file request to a records center terminal or actually interface with COM, CAR, or document imaging systems to retrieve the desired document image.

Packages designed for personal computers start at $100. The mid-range systems cost from $3,000 to $10,000, and extensive mainframe systems may cost $100,000 or more. Aside from the typical hardware configurations, some systems are set up to work with bar code readers and printers, color printers, and networks.

Program Evaluation

Regular and formal program evaluation is a good management practice. The records staff conducts its own evaluations for purposes of program development, management, and training activities. Program elements and practices are modified as necessary based on established criteria for program success and on changing opportunities to make improvements through the use of new technologies and materials.

Continuing efforts to be responsive to changing user needs will involve feedback from the records users. Opportunities for records user feedback come in the form of on-site visits, customer satisfaction surveys, personal interviews, data analysis, cost studies and more. In addition, an annual retention review by the legal, accounting, and user departments may be used to update retention periods based on new laws and regulations, records usage, and other factors.

More formal audits or compliance reviews may be conducted on an annual basis. Audits best demonstrate top management commitment to the records program when enforcement of program compliance is a driving force behind the audit. The records manager normally determines standards and evaluation criteria to be used by the audit staff. Suggested areas for evaluation include:

- accurate, legible labeling on equipment and media containers that complies with any established standard
- implementation of check-out procedures
- customer satisfaction, as determined by established criteria
- currency of information systems indexes
- conformity with uniform filing systems and filing rules
- compliance with records disposition procedures

Program evaluation reports and audits are used for status reports to top management and to solicit or justify management action. They also become part of the records program documentation.

13

The Challenges Ahead

Information is becoming more critical to the success of a business. Reporting requirements are becoming increasingly demanding. The business information database is growing and evolving in complexity.

The mechanisms to gather and distribute information have been made easier, and they continue to improve. We have better and faster computers, microfilm equipment, and photocopiers. Communications networks are moving information faster to more destinations in today's global economy. Office technologies and the information explosion are impacting how we do business today and tomorrow, but our information systems are out of control.

We do not necessarily need more information. What we need is better information selectivity and accessibility to that information. We are spending more time chasing information than using it to manage our businesses well. We must learn how to organize and control these vast masses of information as we simultaneously create the mechanisms to gather more information.

Until we can sort the good from the bad, it will be difficult to use our records and information to their fullest potential for helping achieve business success. If we are not capable of recalling and analyzing our information at will, or storing it securely and economically, we might be better off without it.

BETTER INFORMATION AT LOWER COSTS

Easy-to-use and effective information systems are required to support business as it faces new challenges and opportunities. These systems enable a timely response to changing business conditions and the changing expectations of a wide range of constituents. But the mounting burden of legal and administrative tasks is overwhelming the typical business. As corporate America attempts to streamline for global competitiveness, we seek relief from our laborious information systems.

Laws and Regulations

The Office of Management and Budget (OMB) estimates that federal regulations in 1990 cost the economy $185 billion, or $1,700 for every taxpayer. The public devoted more than 5.3 billion hours to paperwork. Contributing to this burden are the efforts necessary to keep up with constantly changing laws and regulations.

The authority for the 1980 Paperwork Reduction Act lapsed in 1989. This act empowered the OMB to review federal agency regulations that impose paperwork requirements on the public to determine their necessity and clarity, and any redundancy or excessive burden. It also asked that any records retention requirement of more than three years be justified, unless the records are related to health or taxes. At the time of this writing, proponents of the resurrection of this act are attempting to fill a loophole. When the Supreme Court ruled that the law applied only to information supplied to the government, federal agencies redrafted their regulations so that third parties were required to collect the information for them. Though the OMB could have done a better job of assessing the impact of legislation on paperwork, its efforts were better than no efforts at all.

Record-keeping and retention requirements in existing laws continue to be unreasonably difficult to find and interpret. A number of uniform laws exist in an attempt to reduce and clarify government record-keeping requirements, but not all states have adopted them, which complicates matters for businesses operating in more than one state. Redundant paperwork also could be eliminated by more interagency sharing of basic information.

The technological revolution has sparked new concerns regarding privacy and rules of evidence. Privacy issues are being raised regarding the collection and distribution of information through electronic databases, networks, and electronic mail systems.

Rules of evidence have not yet specifically addressed electronic records and records of other new and developing technologies. Statutes, regulations, and uniform laws also will need to be updated to clarify requirements for computer, optical disk, voice, and other forms of records that are maintained. There is a need for additional case law before people will be completely comfortable with the use of such new record forms in court.

There will be changes on the international front from the European Community and elsewhere regarding intellectual properties. Intellectual property laws in the United States need to undergo dramatic changes to address more clearly computer programs, digitized sounds and images, and more. Patent and copyright laws must be clarified on computer software. One of the dilemmas affecting the business environment is that the intellectual property laws are on a collision course with badly needed software industry standards.

Both the civil justice and criminal justice systems are crying out for reform. Needed are better legislation and enforcement of existing criminal laws that protect business. The civil justice system reform movement underway in the nineties hopes to see better writing of legislation so that it does not create unnecessary litigation. Also addressed will be abusive demands during pretrial fact finding in civil suits.

New Information Systems and Technologies

Technological applications permit us to compress time, improve productivity, and increase profitability. Technologies also impact the way we create, process, communicate, and store information. New information-sharing capabilities are revolutionizing the way an enterprise operates as it tears down barriers and allows a business to get closer to its customers, suppliers, and competitors.

Better management of information processing provides the opportunity to flatten out the organization for decision-making at lower levels. Decentralized management allows a more timely response to changing business conditions. Corporate America's tasks can be accomplished in an employee's home or in a suburban satellite office. In the not-so-distant future, we will be able to create, process, produce, and communicate images, data, voice, and video, without having to leave our desks or homes.

Yet even as we reach out to office technologies to reduce our record-keeping burdens, the road to tomorrow's office environment appears to be a rocky one. Technologies may improve the processing and distribution of information, but they also contribute to certain burdens of managing information. It sometimes takes too much time, effort, and money for an organization to profitably exploit its computer systems. Difficulties originate from inadequate standards and from the end users themselves.

- The tremendous growth in the volume of records and the number of different information systems is overwhelming our ability to maintain information currency and accessibility.

- New technical products may be rushed to market with deficiencies, and something else will be released to take their place before someone is able to work out the kinks.

- The lack of adequate industry and corporate standards prohibits interconnectivity of all information systems for the highest return on investments.

- Knowledge workers are experiencing gaps between a technology's capabilities and its actual use because they lack the necessary know-how or because processes have not been redesigned to realize its full potential.

In the race to adopt new technologies, we are not always careful to use the technologies to automate a more efficient approach to doing business. Automation sometimes results in the ability to work faster—but not smarter. If internal processes are not improved before tackling installation of a new technology, an organization is simply automating inefficiencies in an expensive way.

Office technologies are only a means to an end. Business often turns to office automation as a panacea, desperately wanting to believe in vendors' claims of solving their records problems. Without an appropriate infrastructure, a technology may not be able to provide what is really required by end users, customers, the government, and the courts.

Recorded information—be it electronic, microfilm, or paper—is a fact of life. The concept of a paperless office is a catchy one, but it is not anything we will see in our lifetime. In spite of all the money spent to date on computer office products, more than 80 percent of business information today remains in sight-readable form—paper and microform. The information age and revolutionary developments in office technologies continue to contribute to the rising tide of office paper as much as—or more than—they have eliminated them.

One of the greatest challenges facing most businesses today is a game of catch-up regarding their records and information. The evolution from a paper-based to multi-media information systems has resulted in a loss of control over information—if it was ever controlled in the first place. Existing systems do not always function well on their own, and most systems are not connected to other systems, or they are unable to function well with other systems.

The introduction of new technologies on top of existing information systems will mandate the integration of text, data, graphics, images, and voice. Because technologies have only begun to pervade our office environment, interconnectivity standards have yet to be developed. More often than not, every new information system impacts another system by adding to its volume or otherwise complicating it. And instead of working in concert with other systems to support an organization's information needs, most systems are spinning off in their own directions.

- Early computer systems produced warehouses full of large paper printouts.

- Document imaging systems keep a large volume of information available at a computer terminal, but not all original paper documents can be eliminated, because of their legal value.

- Microfilm users are not always able to assume that they have the most current and accurate version of information that also is available in paper files and on computers.

Toward a Coordinated Approach

To harness the power of information, we must organize and integrate our various information systems. No single information system today is capable of providing all of the information solutions and support services required by business. Compatible and connected systems are necessary for the fluidity of information throughout an organization. An enterprise-wide system must be designed so that it is easy to use, easy to manage, and easy to change.

There are tremendous opportunities when paper, microform, and computer systems are coordinated for cost-effective information management solutions. The necessity for interoperability in records and information systems is much like that in computer systems. Standards applied within and across the broad spectrum of information systems will enhance the effectiveness of those systems, both separately and collectively. It only makes sense to gain control of today's information systems before voice, video, and other new systems are added to the mix.

Information systems that continue to operate independently of each other are only one of a number of business traditions contributing to fragmented records management efforts. The piecemeal approach to records management also is perpetuated when records continue to be treated as the private reserve of a specific function, department, or individual employee.

Departments tend to be concerned about their own records, with little consideration of how they fit into the grand scheme of things. Unfortunately, many of the people putting together information today are not trained in its selection and organization. They no doubt have knowledge and expertise in their subject field, but they may not always know:

- what information is available and how to obtain it
- the true value(s) of information
- what record form is most appropriate for users, preservation, and legal compliance
- how to efficiently store and access the information

When individual departments do not comply with a corporate records program, legal and security issues are not always addressed, and media often are poorly chosen.

The House of Good Intentions marketing department generates a variety of records, but it does not participate in the corporate records management program. The department maintains an excessive number of duplicate records that are available in other departments. It has no established filing system, so it may be difficult to find the records necessary when a product liability suit is filed or when the company prepares for a centennial celebration. Department employees are not thoroughly trained on how to protect marketing and pricing strategies, which exist in a number of record forms. They also frequently file correspondence that affects customer agreements without informing the law department of those legal documents.

Information managers tend to focus on the mechanics of a specific function or on an individual information system. The real focus should be on an enterprise-wide information system. In place of unspoken rivalries between data processing, records, and other information management functions, there should be a partnership working together on records and information.

One corporation has a records manager, MIS director, microfilm specialist, and an archivist. There is no central index for records under the control of all of these managers, so end users must search in more than one place to locate information needed. The archivist is frustrated because important corporate history is on personal and mainframe computers, out of his control and preservation efforts. The records manager is responsible for only paper records and has no idea of what information is duplicated on computers or microfilm. The MIS director is not aware of legal retention requirements for mainframe computer information, and she has no control over information on personal computers.

A comprehensive records and information management program focuses on a number of program elements as they apply to all information carriers, and at every stage of their life cycles. The absence of a single program element may affect another program element, or it may result in business losses and liabilities.

- Without a retention schedule, valueless records may be converted to an expensive record form for ongoing consumption of company resources.
- Without indexing, critical information cannot be efficiently retrieved, or it may not be retrieved at all.
- Without information security, a company may experience a loss of rights or revenues.

A NEW LOOK FOR RECORDS AND INFORMATION MANAGEMENT

Records and information management means different things to different people. Traditional perceptions do not accurately describe the evolving roles of records and information in business. To make way for a new way of thinking, records management myths must be dispelled. Among those myths are:

- We will not need records management in a paperless office.
- We must keep all records in case we are sued.

- Records management is a fancy name for records centers.
- Optical disk is the answer to records management problems.
- Records management means paper filing and storage.
- Individual departments know best what to do with their records.
- Only old records can be destroyed.
- Personal files are not a business concern.
- A fire, flood, or employee sabotage won't happen here.
- Records are not a risk management or MIS concern.
- Anyone can manage a records and information program.

We often get hung up on the word "record," which today encompasses far more than the obvious paper documents. Record-keeping requirements do not go away when information is digitized. Ongoing issues related to all record forms include:

- compliance with laws and regulations
- confidentiality and security
- costs and efficiencies
- evidentiary procedures
- permanence and durability
- retention and destruction
- retrieval and storage
- support and services for end users

Business in general is not doing as good a job of managing all of its various records and information as it could—or should. Some companies have policies, but no compliance, and others have no policies. Most companies address selected aspects of records management by policy enforcement, but they neglect the big picture of how all program elements may work together for improved efficiencies and effectiveness.

Misunderstanding of what proper records management can do for a business contributes to a gap between the function's capabilities and its actual applications. One major reason why records management does not have the respect it deserves is inadequate support from top management. Unable to fully comprehend or appreciate the benefits and issues, top management withholds resources from this important business function.

It is not always easy to visualize the advantages when we have been doing it wrong for so long. Most executives do not see the staff struggling in the trenches to maintain and access records. Or they may not recognize the connection between information and business strategies. For some executives, only a crisis will alert them to the fact that an important business activity may have been ignored for too long.

Most records and information management benefits are intangible. A records management program is a hard sell to all levels of an organization, but it is possible to obtain some figures related to cost reductions.

The House of Good Intentions was able to quantify savings in one year of $1 million in space, equipment, and supplies as a direct result of its records and information management activities. Not measured were the benefits from improved productivity and better customer service.

We need more and better ways to quantify and measure savings, cost avoidance, management effectiveness, and other program benefits.

- Methods to quantify white-collar productivity are few and far between. Evaluation of the impact of records and information management on that productivity is even more elusive.
- The effects of the availability or unavailability of information in a timely manner are difficult to measure.
- No one can predict if an organization will fall victim to criminal actions or a natural disaster.
- Not only is it impossible to know what litigation or government investigation looms in the future, the consequences of too few or too many records cannot always be predicted.

Records management faces a difficult task of garnering adequate support when it cannot present a strong case amid stiff competition for a company's limited resources. Expertise, staffing, and dollars continue to be allocated to other business activities. It is ironic that such a large portion of those scarce resources is allocated to computer systems when the largest proportion of information continues to exist in paper and microfilm forms.

Records and information represent assets, or they are assets in their own right. They also are a strategic resource for management effectiveness and loss prevention. As a vital corporate resource, they should be managed and controlled much like other more visible and better-understood resources—land, labor, and capital. Records management is a corporate cost of doing business, similar to the accounting, insurance, and litigation functions. We can pay a little now, or we can pay a lot more later when business losses occur as a result of poor record-keeping practices.

Records and information management is being redefined as it affects all business functions both separately and as a whole. It must cross interdepartmental lines to be effective, and its success or failure impacts an entire organization. The time is long overdue for this back-room operation to move into a more visible position in the organization.

Records activities today tend to be scattered throughout the organization and are not coordinated by any single individual or department. Records management must move toward a coordinating and facilitating function and away from a disjointed collection of file folders, computer tapes, and storage facilities.

Toward a Chief Information Officer

In the absence of top management commitment, underqualified records managers are hired, or no records manager is hired at all. Some records managers may lack the skills necessary to sell a program to management, or they are not empowered with the authority and resources to manage a program well. Not all records managers today recognize the broad scope of records and information management, or they lack the expertise necessary to manage a comprehensive program.

Management of multimedia information systems is far more sophisticated and complicated than simply managing paper filing systems. Today's records manager must keep up with the latest in:

- relevant legal considerations
- office technologies
- information management products and methods

Instead of being locked into a narrow technical perspective, the new manager must consider how records and information management practices will support, protect, and add value to an enterprise. Government requirements and an increasingly litigious climate contribute to new record-keeping requirements and a necessity to focus more on record content than on record form.

These necessities for a focus on content and on information systems compatibility dictate a single authority at the highest levels of the organization. As business installs more information technologies, a chief information officer (CIO) will find a place in the organizational structure.

The CIO must be involved in corporate planning so that information systems will fully support the organization and so that the organization can fully exploit its information systems capabilities. This manager will need to develop and maintain close working relationships with other departments. Empire building is out and partnerships are in for developing an effective information management program.

REALIZING CHANGE

From adding new product lines to installation of new technologies, business is always in a state of change. Just as the installation of new technologies provides new capabilities for change, so does a records and information management program. And like new technologies, it also may require changes in the way a company does business. These changes will cost in terms of financial, human, and other resources.

Corporate change normally originates at the top and works its way down through every level of the organization. But the records manager often becomes squeezed between the order issuer and the records users and their managers, who are unwilling to change their ways. Nothing can be accomplished until executives empower others to take action. That commitment must be visible enough to get the attention of line managers and end users throughout the entire organization. Continued top management support is necessary for a program to remain viable and responsive to business and user needs.

The level of commitment to change is a determining factor for the success of records management. Forces that are restraining change may be a general resistance to change, a lack of confidence in records systems, and a shortage of resources. Commitment to change depends on the:

- degree of knowledge and understanding of the change
- level of dissatisfaction with the status quo
- desirability of the proposed end state
- practicality and costs of the change

The driving forces behind records and information management changes will be program support and education, communications, and rewards systems. There are a number of key players who will be responsible for the methods and systems redesign that will be necessary to implement a comprehensive records program. Today, those players are working independently of each other throughout the organization. These change agents must begin to work together for a clear understanding of business goals, and of the business processes required to reach those goals. They must determine the roles of records and information in the company's mission and the ways in which they may successfully support and help advance the organization's winning strategies.

If we do not maintain a proper business focus to regain control of our records and information, we will end up with expensive information systems of no real productive value. A cohesive, well-thought-out information system must become an integral part of how a business defines itself. Through better information processing and distribution, the system will transform an otherwise burdensome business activity into a competitive weapon.

Everyone is preoccupied with today's tasks and profit margins, but we cannot ignore records and information management issues. A crisis of low productivity, burdensome litigation, or a fire could be too costly. A new vigor will be needed to cast away old habits and to exercise the self-discipline that is necessary in any well-run business. It is not a question of if, but a question of when and how we regain control of our business information systems. There is no better time than now to start a program or dust off an existing one.

The enterprise that masters installation of workable records and information systems is likely to gain strategic advantages in today's highly competitive and litigious marketplace. At the very least, it will avoid senseless disadvantages and possible disaster.

Glossary

AIIM. Association for Information Management.

Active record. A record referenced on a regular basis during the normal course of business, such as current invoices, personnel records, correspondence, or reports on current projects.

Admissibility. A characteristic of evidence that enables it to be introduced in a court proceeding.

Admission. A statement made by one party in litigation that is relevant to the cause of an adversarial party because it is against the interests of the owning party and is presumed to be true because it is that party's own statement of fact.

Adverse inference. A finding by a court through a reasoning process that information in records that were inappropriately destroyed by a party is unfavorable to that party, even though the information was not available to the court.

Archival record. A record that is to be preserved for an extended period of time, such as a historical record.

ARMA International. Association of Records Managers and Administrators International. (4200 Somerset Drive, Suite 215, Prairie Village, KS, 66208, 1-800-422-2762) offers a number of publications for the records management professional, including a quarterly professional journal, books, reports, videos, slides, and transparencies on the following topics: industry standards, filing, records center operations, disaster prevention and recovery, recovery of water-damaged records, business forms, microform and optical disk systems, records management computer systems, legal records, and much more.

Attorney-client privilege. The right of a client or an attorney to refuse to disclose and to prevent any other person from disclosing confidential communications between the client and the attorney.

Audit hold. The procedure to halt destruction of records when it is determined that an audit is foreseeable or pending.

Authentication. The determination of the genuineness, reliability, or trustworthiness of evidence.

Business records organization chart. A method of classifying records by functional and subject categories for indexing, organizing, filing, and retrieval of records, as well as assignment of record retention periods. More commonly referred to as a file structure.

Civil case. A court proceeding to determine and enforce rights between parties, to prevent future rights violations, and to provide appropriate damages or compensation.

Computer assisted retrieval (CAR) system. A records system that films and encodes documents for indexing by computer.

Computer output microfilm (COM). An original record produced directly from computer data onto microfilm.

Computer record. A form of record generated by data stored in electronic or magnetic form on a computer.

Confidential record. A record or information that is shared only on a need-to-know basis and that its owner or subject does not want freely disclosed or used by others without prior permission. Confidential information encompasses various types of private, technical, financial, business, and customer information. The term confidential is sometimes used to describe proprietary information.

Conservation. Processes and actions to retard or control the deterioration of a record form or medium.

Contract. A mutual agreement between two or more parties that creates, modifies, or dissolves a legal relationship between the parties.

Copy Management. A management function that controls the duplication of records and their duplication devices to ensure effective and economical creation of duplicate records.

Copyright. The legal right granted to an author, composer, playwright, publisher, or distributor to exclusive publication, production, sale, or distribution of a literary, musical, dramatic, or artistic work, including computer software.

Custodial capacity. A relationship in which one party has the responsibility to protect property in its possession that is owned by another.

Data. A general term used to denote any or all facts, numbers, letters and symbols that refer to or describe an object, transaction, event, condition, and so on. Most frequently used in reference to information contained on a computer.

Designated record copy. An original or duplicate record that is the record to be retained and protected according to a record retention schedule.

Destruction. The process of totally obliterating information on a record by making the information unreadable or unusable.

Destruction suspension. The procedure to halt routine and other destruction of records when it is determined that those records may be relevant to foreseeable or pending litigation, government investigation, or audit.

Discovery. The legal process that allows parties involved in a legal proceeding to obtain records and information relevant to the proceeding that are in the possession of another party.

Dispersal. The process of placing copies of vital records in locations other than those housing the originals.

Disposition. An action taken on a record, such as transfer, conversion to another medium, or destruction.

Documentation. The creation of records to describe an event or act, and to show compliance with a policy, procedure, or process.

Document production. The process of retrieving and producing a record for use in a government investigation or a legal proceeding.

Duplicate record. A reproduction of an original record by means of photography, mechanical or electronic rerecording, chemical reproduction, or other techniques that accurately reproduce the original.

Electronic imaging system. A computer-based technology that scans a document image and stores it in electronic form for retrieval.

Fiduciary capacity. A relationship in which one party is responsible for the management of the financial matters and records of another party.

File management. A management function that provides for the analysis of filing equipment to determine the most efficient type for a given operation at the most economical price, and to establish a method of indexing and arranging records.

File structure. A method of classifying records by functional and subject categories for indexing, organizing, filing, and retrieval of records, as well as assignment of record retention periods.

Filing system. A method of organizing and storing physical records and information for easy retrieval.

Foreseeable. The reasonable anticipation that an activity or event, such as litigation, investigation, or audit, will occur in the future.

Forms management. A management function that assures that valueless forms do not exist and that necessary forms are designed, produced, and distributed economically and efficiently.

Freedom of Information Act (FOIA). A federal law that requires public disclosure of the records, opinions, findings, policies, and procedures of federal agencies, with the exception of information that is privileged, confidential, or classified.

Inactive record. A record that is not referenced in the course of normal business activities, but is retained because it contains information of real or potential use or value.

Indexing system. A method of categorizing and encoding records for efficient organization, storage, retrieval, and processing.

Information carrier. A general term to describe a record medium or record form.

Information disclosure. The act of providing a record or information to another party.

Information processor. A mechanical or electronic means to transmit, convert, or manipulate data, information, or records.

Information resources. Records, publications, electronic information databases, and other sources of data and information.

Information security program. A component of a records and information program that establishes methods and procedures to protect sensitive and valuable records from loss, damage, or unauthorized disclosure.

Information security threat. A condition, event, or action that may lead to damage, loss, or unauthorized disclosure of records and information.

Intellectual property. The protected expressions of scientific, artistic, or other creative and/or commercial endeavors; a special type of intangible personal property arising from the creative endeavors of the human mind and research, generally patents, copyrights, trademarks, trade names, or service marks.

Jukebox. A computer device that stores and retrieves optical disks.

Legal considerations. Various laws, regulations, and rules of evidence (and their interpretations) that affect rights and responsibilities regarding record-keeping.

Legal hold. The procedure to halt destruction of records related to foreseeable or pending litigation or government investigation.

Life cycle. The time period from the creation of a record and its active use through its ultimate disposition, whether archiving or destruction.

Limitation of action. See **Statute of limitations**.

Limitation of assessment. The period of time after a tax return is filed or the tax becomes due during which the taxing agency can determine or modify the amount of taxes owed.

Machine-sensible record. A term used by the Internal Revenue Service to indicate computer-readable data or a record that is not visible but that is accessible with appropriate equipment.

Maintain (maintenance). The actions necessary to retain and preserve a record.

Media management and integration program. A component of a records and information management program that controls the forms or media of records, and provides a system or methodology to index and organize all existing record forms into a uniform records and information system that is media-transparent and treats all record forms alike for purposes of records retrieval, retention, and disposition.

Medium (Media). The material or substance on which data or information is recorded, such as paper, optical disk, magnetic tape, microfilm, photograph, and so on. Also referred to as a record form or an information carrier.

Microform. The generic name for any of the various forms in which the use of microphotography reproduces a record. A microform may be microfilm rolls or cartridges, microfiche, film jackets, aperture cards, and so on.

Name authority. A standardized method of formatting personal, government, and corporate names to facilitate data manipulation, filing, and retrieval of information. The use of name authority ensures that information on the same person or entity is indexed under a single name instead of under a number of variations representing a single person or organization.

Need to know. A requirement for access to, knowledge of, or possession of confidential information in order to perform tasks or services essential to the fulfillment of job responsibilities.

Nondisclosure agreement. A written contract between two parties wherein one or both parties agree not to disclose certain information to other parties.

Obstruction of justice. A deliberate act to interfere with a government investigation or judicial proceeding.

Office of record. The group, department, or office responsible for maintaining a designated record copy.

Optical disk. A record form that is created by the use of laser optic technology.

Original record. A newly created document, recording, or record intended to be considered the same as an original under rules of evidence, including a printout or other sight-readable output of computer data that can be shown to accurately reflect the data or information.

Patent. A grant made by the federal government to an inventor that assures the exclusive right to make, use, and sell a new and useful design, process, machine, manufactured item, or other composition, or any new and useful improvement on it. The concrete expression of a novel and useful idea or design is protected for a limited period of time prescribed by statute.

Permanence and durability. The characteristics of a record form that determine its ability to withstand use, abuse, adverse environmental conditions, and aging.

Personal record. A record belonging to an individual that has no content relevant to the business, was not produced using resources of the business, and has no place in the business environment.

Preservation (preserve). The process and actions to maintain and protect a record for as long as it is needed, including efforts to retard or control deterioration of the record form and to prevent loss of the record.

Private record. A record or information about an individual or business that must not be disclosed without proper authorization. Frequently referred to as a confidential record. Private information includes, but is not limited to, employee or customer records, attorney-client privileged records, and so forth.

Proprietary information. Information, knowledge, data, and know-how to which a company owns rights. Proprietary information includes patent applications, trade secrets, and technical, financial, or commercial information that would be of benefit to competitors.

Record. Any form of recorded information that is created or maintained for use at a later time, including but not limited to paper, photographs, negatives, microfilm, maps, drawings, charts, cards, magnetic tapes, software, motion pictures, videos, optical disks, and microfiches.

Record conversion. The process of changing a record from one medium or form to another.

Record form. See **Medium**.

Record-keeping. Actions and processes related to the creation, maintenance, form(s), protection, and disposition of records.

Record-keeping requirements. Policies, laws, regulations, and practices related to the record-keeping functions that are based on business needs, government requirements, and other legal considerations.

Records and information management. A management function that systematically controls the life cycle of all records from creation or receipt through processing, distribution, maintenance, protection, and retrieval to their ultimate disposition. The process includes filing systems, media management and integration, records retention and disposition, vital records protection, and other functions. Activities are designed to promote economies and efficiencies, to assure that needless records are not created or maintained, and to assure that valuable records are maintained, protected, and made easily accessible to users.

Records center. A room or building devoted to the proper storage and protection of records.

Record series. A group of similar or related records that normally are used or filed as a unit. The group or category is the product of an official function or activity and permits the evaluation of records as a unit for retention scheduling, control, storage, and other purposes.

Records manager. A knowledgeable individual designated to control the records management program.

Reports management. A management function that assures that valueless reports do not exist and that necessary reports are well presented, accurate and timely.

Retention period. The period of time during which records must be maintained in a certain location or form because they are needed for operational, legal, fiscal, historical, or other purposes. A retention period may be stated in terms of months or years, and sometimes is expressed as contingent upon the occurrence of an event.

Retention program. A component of a records and information management program that controls the creation, maintenance, and ultimate disposition of records at the appropriate time.

Retention schedule. A document prepared as part of a records retention program that lists the periods of time needed to maintain records in active status in a certain form, location, and so on, up to final disposition of archiving or destruction.

Risk management. A management function or process that analyzes the costs, risks, and benefits of alternatives in order to determine the most desirable alternative.

ROM. A term describing a computer record as "read only memory," indicating that the record may be read, but not be added to, modified, or deleted.

Security copying. The process of duplicating a record as a method of ensuring the continued existence of the recorded information.

Semi-active record. A record referenced occasionally in the course of conducting normal business.

Sensitive record. A record that must not be disclosed indiscriminately to others because of the nature of the information.

Service mark. A distinctive symbol, word, letter, number, picture, or combination thereof adopted and used by a business to identify its services and to distinguish them from the services of others.

Software. Statements or logic in any form, medium, or language, intended as instructions for machine processing, including codes, related documentation, user manuals, and other descriptive material related to programming procedures, techniques, or principles.

Statute of limitations. A statute prescribing limitations to the right of action on certain described causes of action or criminal prosecutions; the time period after an event or from which a right begins, during which a legal action or lawsuit may be initiated. Also referred to as limitation of actions.

Subpoena duces tecum. A court order requiring a witness to appear in court, produce relevant records in his possession or control, and provide testimony.

Tax hold. The procedure to halt destruction of records related to a foreseeable or pending tax agency review of returns and tax records.

Trademark. A distinctive symbol, word, letter, number, picture, or combination thereof adopted and used by a merchant or manufacturer to distinguish and identify its goods. May be registered under state and federal laws. A trademark seeks to guarantee a product's quality and creates and sustains a demand for the product.

Trade name. A distinctive name that may serve as a trademark or service mark but is used to designate the business entity itself.

Trade secret. Any formula, pattern, device, know-how, or compilation of information that provides an advantage over competitors who do not know or use it. Trade secret laws prohibit others from wrongfully breaching such secrecy through the commission of a tort or the violation of an express or implied contract.

Trustworthiness. The degree to which evidence may be relied on as being what it claims to be.

Uniform laws. Laws prepared by the National Conference of Commissioners on Uniform State Laws in an effort to establish consistencies among the states.

Uniform laws that affect record-keeping in business include the Uniform Business Records as Evidence Act, Uniform Preservation of Private Business Records Act, Uniform Photographic Copies of Business and Public Records as Evidence Act, and Uniform Rules of Evidence.

Valuable record. A record that represents a tangible or intangible asset or that affects the income, losses, or profits of a business.

Visible record. A form of record for which the image is visible directly by sight or with the assistance of magnification.

Vital record. A record essential to the preservation, continuation, and protection of a company, its rights, employees, customers, shareholders, and business in general. A vital record is necessary for resumption and/or continuation of operations; for the re-creation of the legal and financial status of the company; for the fulfillment of obligations to stockholders, employees, and/or outside interests.

Vital records center. A facility devoted to the storage and protection of vital records.

Vital records program. A component of a records and information management program that manages the protection of vital records from damage or loss.

Vital records schedule. A document prepared as part of the vital records program that lists vital records and how they are to be protected.

WORM. A term describing a computer record as "write once, read many times," indicating that the record may be created, but not be added to, modified, or deleted.

Bibliography

Allen, Michael. "Cleaning House: U.S. Companies Pay Increasing Attention to Destroying Files." *Wall Street Journal* (September 2, 1987).

Austin, Robert B. "10,000,000 Reasons for Records Management." *Records Management Quarterly* (July 1985).

Business Laws, Inc. *Guide to Records Retention: The Lawyer's Role.* Cleveland, OH: Business Laws, Inc., 1991.

Clark, Jesse L. *The Encyclopedia of Records Retention.* Northfield, IL: The Records Management Group, 1990.

Diamond, Susan Z. *Records Management: A Practical Guide.* New York: American Management Associations, Publications Group (AMACOM), 1983.

Diebold, John. *Managing Information: The Challenge and the Opportunity.* New York: AMACOM, 1985.

Diers, Fred. "Paper-Based Files Remain a Fact of Business Life." *The Office* (July 1990).

Dykemann, John B. "Software that Manages Your Files." *Modern Office Technology* (February 1991).

Emery, James C. *Management Information Systems: The Critical Strategic Resource.* New York: Oxford University Press, 1987.

Fedders, John M., and Lauryn H. Guttenplan. "Document Retention and Destruction: Practical, Legal and Ethical Considerations." *The Notre Dame Lawyer* (October 1980).

Fernberg, Patricia M. "The Economics that Drive Mobile Storage." *Modern Office Technology* (August 1987).

Gureasko, H. Russell. "The Records Management Professional—Out of the File Room, into the Executive Suite." *Records Management Quarterly* (October 1978).

Lane, Marc J. *Legal Handbook for Small Business.* New York: AMACOM, rev. ed. 1989.

"Less Litigation, More Justice." *Wall Street Journal* (August 14, 1991).

Leyzorek, Michael. "Legal and Ethical Responsibilities: A Missing Feature in Some Records Management Systems." *Records Management Quarterly* (January 1991).

Marchand, Donald A., and Forest W. Horton, Jr. *Infotrends: Profiting From Your Information Resources.* New York: John Wiley and Sons, 1986.

Morgan, Dennis F., and Maryanne Nawoczenski. "Memory Loss: Combatting Corporate Senility." *Records Management Quarterly* (July 1985).

Murray, John M. "Legal Considerations in Records Management." *Records Management Quarterly* (January 1978).

Murray, Toby. "Don't Get Caught With Your Plans Down . . . " *Records Management Quarterly* (April 1987).

Parker, Donn B. *Fighting Computer Crime.* New York: Charles Scribner's Sons, 1983.

Phillips, John T., and Albin Wagner. *Software Directory for Automated Records Management.* Prairie Village, KS: ARMA International, 1990.

"Preservation of Information." *The Records & Retrieval Report* 2.3 (March 1986).

"Records Management Priorities of the 90s." *Modern Office Technology* (February 1990).

"A Records Management Program for the Information Age." *Modern Office Technology* (September 1991).

Rumer, Thomas A. "Corporate History and the Records Manager." *Records Management Quarterly* (October 1986).

Sampson, Karen L. "All Those Business Records!" *South Metro Denver Business* (Fall 1990).

———. "Computer Viruses: Not Fads, Not Funny." *The Office* (October 1989).

———. "Poor Records Management Batters the Bottom Line." *The Office* (March 1989).

———. "Power Problems Can Be Minimized by Controls." *The Office* (February 1990).

———. "Records Management: The Legal Aspects." *The Office* (April 1990).

Skupsky, Donald S. "Legal Liability of the Records and Information Management Professional." *Records Management Quarterly* (April 1987).

———. *Legal Requirements for Business Records: Federal Requirements and State Requirements.* Denver: Information Requirements Clearinghouse, updated annually.

_____. *Recordkeeping Requirements*. Denver: Information Requirements Clearinghouse, 1989.

Smith, Lee. "Trial Lawyers Face a New Charge." *Fortune* (August 26, 1991).

Waegemann, C. Peter. *Handbook of Record Storage and Space Management*. Westport, CT: Quorum Books, 1985.

_____. "Legal Issues in Records Management." *The Records & Retrieval Report* 1.7 (September 1985).

_____. "Optical Disk Technology and How to Implement It." *The Office* (October 1990).

Weise, Carl E. "Records Management: The Management Science Too Long Ignored." *Records Management Quarterly* (April 1986).

Wolff, Richard E. "Snap, Crackle and Pop." *Records Management Quarterly* (April 1985).

Wormwald, Karen. "Rid Your Records of Photocopy Waste." *The Office* (July 1990).

Index

About the Author

KAREN L. SAMPSON is the owner of Scenarios by Sampson, a business consulting firm. A former corporate records manager, she now consults with clients on a number of records management issues. She has also developed customized computer systems to track business records and has designed records centers. Her publications in business magazines include articles on records and information management.